BULLSHIT!

AND LIES

Other works by this author:

You're Not Nuts... You've Just Got Issues. Outskirts Press, Parker, CO, 2006.

For Parents & Teens: A Guide To Peaceful Coexistence. Outskirts Press, Parker, CO, 2007.

Them There Guys: An Epistolary Odyssey. With David B. Finkelstein. Lulu Press, 2010.

Selfonomics: How Broadly-defined Self-Interest Explains Everything!. ttgPress, 2014.

Essays. With David B. Finkelstein. ttgPress, 2015.

The Legacy Book: A Guided (Auto)biography. 2017, ttgPress.

When Technology And Self-Interest Collide: (Watch Out!). ttgPress, 2017.

Them There Eyes: And The Woman Behind Them. ttgPress, 2017.

I An An Echo Chamber: The Basis Of Tribalism,. ttgPress, 2018.

BULLSHIT!

AND LIES

Anthony J. Gribin, Ph.D.

ttgPress 2018

First Printing: 2018

ISBN 978-0-9993006-4-0

ttgPress

ajgribin@optonline.net

Dedication

To the truth tellers…

Contents

INTRODUCTION: BULLSHIT RULES!

We, the American people, have been privileged to be exposed to a whole, relatively new, set of words and phrases that have added to the breadth of our vocabulary. The common theme among these pearls is the subject of truth or its absence. For those of us tuned in to the world around us, we've been treated to the likes of:

"alternative facts"
tribalism
factcheck
media as the "enemy of the people"
collusion
alt-right
conspiracy theory
"Believe me"
loser
moron
witch hunt
gaslighting
spearphishing
troll factory
election meddling
hoax
and, of course, "fake news"

1

All of these terms offer, involve or promote, some form of bullshit. As an example, "fake news," or rather "FAKE NEWS!", is pulled out of the bag to explain what a person disagrees with or dislikes, but cannot provide any realistic or cogent counterarguments. It is an all-purpose retort that fits any adverse situation. It is also pure bullshit. More on this later.

Given that we are increasingly exposed to, at best false, at worst imaginary information and arguments, we need to play defense. The aim of this book is help innocent, unsuspecting, gullible suckers like you and me change into astute, suspicious and perceptive consumers of information. It will help all of us stop being chumps, patsies, fools, saps, victims, pushovers and pigeons for anyone who is selling any kind of a message with either an overt or hidden agenda.

The world has changed with the Presidency of Donald Trump. Not that he, alone, is responsible. Barack Obama was a respectable, seemingly upstanding and honest man (for a politician), whose presidency nonetheless divided the country into factions. Hillary Clinton, seen as "four more years of Obama" led to a backlash against Democrats, especially in parts of the country that were suffering financially as a result of job displacement, income inequality and immigration policies. Donald Trump, running on promises to undo everything that came before him, ran a brilliant and unorthodox campaign, both in the primaries and in the general election and, in the end, was victorious.

Whether one agrees or disagrees with the *content* of the policies that he represented, the way he spoke and behaved was different from anything that came before. He is/was, to be blunt, the biggest liar and bullshitter the country has ever seen. Not only did he play fast and loose with the truth, he did it with the panache of a media star; a master at stagecraft and showmanship. His act is largely made up of bullshit and lies. There is little doubt as to the magnitude of his dishonesty.

> "The Washington Post's Fact-Checker blog has been keeping a strict count of President Donald Trump's many misstatements, untruths and outright lies. And, over the weekend at a rally in Michigan, Trump hit a(nother) milestone: He topped 3,000 untrue or misleading statements in 466 days in office.
>
> That means that, on average, Trump says 6.5 things that aren't true a day. Every. Single. Day. Trump is actually picking up the pace when it comes to not telling the truth; he has averaged nine untruths or

misleading statements a day over the past two months, according to the Post's count."[1]

In addition to lying, Trump has also set new standards for bullshitting as well:

"…characterizations of Trump as a liar aren't quite accurate, or at least don't provide the full picture. Trump's comments illustrate instead that he's a full-fledged bullshit artist. There's a difference: Lying involves conscious deception, whereas bullshitting is a more insidious attempt to blur the lines between truth and falsehood.
    In 2015, …Trump, then in the early stages of his presidential campaign, had all the characteristics of a bullshit artist: He not only frequently made false statements, but was indifferent to whether they were false or not. In doing so, he undermines the

---

[1] Cilizza, Chris. "President Trump lied more than 3,000 times in 466 days." CNN Politics, 5/9/18 @https://www.cnn.com/2018/05/01/politics/donald-trump-3000/index.html

very idea that the truth is relevant or even knowable."[2]

The result of this behavior has been to drive the populace further apart into their tribes and individual echo chambers, which either love Trump's style unconditionally or hate it with a passion. To avoid cognitive dissonance, supporters have had to change their attitudes to be in alignment with their love of Trump. As a byproduct, civility has been a casualty, misogynistic and prejudicial behavior has been overlooked, and intellectualism and political correctness have been derided. Quite simply, Trump's ascendance has given license to bad behavior.

Opponents of Trump have had to adapt as well. They simply disbelieve everything that comes out of his mouth. This isn't laudable either, since once in a while, it would be nice to have faith in the leader of your country and the most powerful man in the world.

Bullshit and lies are being pushed at us all the time, even by people with whom we agree. Anti-Trump news media also spew out lies, albeit at a lower frequency and volume than pro-Trump media. Each of us has an echo chamber that perpetuates whatever

[2] Heer, Jeet. "Worse Than a Liar." The New Republic, 3/15/18. @https://newrepublic.com/article/147504/worse-liar-trump-lies-trudeau

beliefs we hold. If we are anti-Trump we only seek information consistent with that belief and avoid dissonant information. How do we know that we're not being lied to or bullshitted by friends with like minds or networks that are vying for eyeballs?

The only defense we can muster is to do more due diligence, read more than one source of news, ask questions, learn what bullshit sounds, looks like and smells like. The more we know about the way bullshitters bullshit, about what tricks are up their sleeves, the better defenses we can muster. The main purpose of this book is to help readers recognize bullshit for what it is…bullshit. Or, to put it another way, since *bullshit rules*, we need some *rules to filter bullshit*.

1: BULLSHIT!

There's an apocryphal anecdote about a round of golf, played in Ireland, in the formative days of the game. Two men, Seamus and Sean, were playing on a primitive course, which was carved out of a cow pasture. They finished the first hole, and as they arrived at number two [sic], Seamus approached his ball to examine his lie. Sean pointed to a brown pile situated a few inches from Seamus' lie and the following conversation ensued:

Sean: Careful Seamus, don't step in the cow shit.

Seamus: "That's bullshit, Sean!

Sean (insulted): Oh yeah? That's a rotten lie, Seamus!

Seamus, "You accuse me of a rotten lie? This, from a guy talking bullshit?[3]

---

[3] The above apocryphal anecdote is an example of complete and utter bullshit.

As a kid growing up in a big city I had to deal with a lot of bullshit. Not the real McCoy, but bullshit through the medium of words. I was too naive to know it at the time, but "bullshit," as a word, is used in three separate ways:

To describe conversation. This is what you are doing when you are talking with "the guys." Girls don't bullshit. They converse, confide in one another and discuss things. Guys bullshit, as in, "We were bullshitting at Phil's house." Or, "We were shooting the shit" at Phil's house." Similar, less profane ways of describing male interactions are "chewing the fat" or "shooting the breeze." Real men prefer to reference bullshit.

As an exclamation. This may be in response to what another guy says, or a reaction to anything you hear (or see on TV) with which you disagree or disbelieve, *as long as you were in the company of other guys*. If a girl, teacher or parent were present you'd find another, less profane way of expressing your disbelief or disagreement, such as "That's nuts!" or "You're off your rocker!"

The primary pronunciation of the word puts the stress on the first syllable, as in BULLshit! Used in this way, it expresses disagreement or disbelief. A secondary meaning can be conveyed by putting the emphasis on the second syllable, as in bullSHIT! This adds an attitude of indignation to the disagreement or disbelief, as in, "How dare you say that?" Or "I can't believe you said that!"

As a verb and act. While the first two meanings are interesting, if this book concerned merely how guys talk to one another, and how the word functions as an expletive, it would be a very short book. Maybe even a pamphlet.

This third and most important use of the word "bullshit" has seen a mercurial rise in recent years, as a near-synonym for lying and/or not speaking the truth. Both lying and bullshitting are used as verbs, as in the acts of bullshitting and lying.

There's an old proverb to the effect, "A lie is halfway around the world before truth has got its boots on."[4] This obvious truism led a deep-thinking Italian computer programmer by the name of Alberto Brandolini to propose the "bullshit asymmetry principle,"[5] which asserts, "The amount of energy needed to refute bullshit is an order of magnitude bigger than to produce it."[6] So not only does bullshit fly, it's hard to

---

[4] Speake, Jennifer. Oxford Dictionary of Proverbs. London, Oxford University Press, 2015 (6th ed.).

[5] Brandolini, Alberto. @ http://ordrespontane.blogspot.fr/2014/07/brandolinis-law.html2

[6] An "order of magnitude bigger" is generally considered to be ten times greater.

shoot down once it's in the air. This is especially true if we don't know what bullshit is and what it is not. All we know it that once out, bullshit spreads quickly through the pasture of life.

Okay, so what exactly is bullshit? While deep thinkers throughout the millennia have wrestled with this conundrum, a perfect example is offered in the monumental Mel Brooks film, "History of the World, Part I." Comicus, played by Brooks in ancient Rome, tries to collect his weekly unemployment insurance money from a clerk, played by Bea Arthur. Here's the interchange:

> Clerk: Occupation?
> Comicus: Stand-up philosopher!
> Clerk: What?
> Comicus: Stand-up philosopher.
> Clerk: (Gives him strange look.)
> Comicus: I coalesce the vapor of human experience into a viable and logical com prehension.
> Clerk: Oh! A BULLSHIT ARTIST!

The statement by Comicus is clearly bullshit. It, like pornography, is hard to define but we know it when we see it[7] (or hear it). Most of the time that is. But is it identical to a lie? The leading thinker on this subject has heretofore been an august Princeton University professor and philosopher by the name of Harry Frankfurt. In his treatise, "On Bullshit,"[8] he avers that they are *not* the same. A liar and a truth teller both reference the truth but the liar seeks to hide it. The bullshitter cares nothing about the truth, only whether he can persuade his audience to buy what he is selling, be it a product or an idea. "His eye is not on the facts at all…. He does not care whether the things he says describe reality correctly. He just picks them out, or makes them up, to suit his purpose."[9]

So if a person knows the truth and tells the truth, he is a truth teller. If he knows the truth, but does not tell the truth, he is a liar. And if he doesn't reference the truth, or doesn't care about what is true, he is a bullshitter.

If the bullshitter doesn't reference the truth, we can surmise certain corollaries to Frankfurt's principle. Let's call them the "The Bullshit Corollaries":

---

[7] Lattman, Stewart. "The Origins of Justice Stewart's "I Know It When I See It." Wall Street Journal, Law Blog, 9/27/07.

[8] Frankfurt, Harry G. On Bullshit. Princeton, N.J.: Princeton University Press, 2005.

[9] ibid.

1) Just about all bullshit is made up of lies. Occasionally, perhaps by accident, the bullshitter will stumble upon the truth, in the same sense that a broken clock is right twice a day. Truth is unintentional.

2) Although all bullshit consist of lies, lies are *not* bullshit. They are calculated and targeted to achieve a certain result. As will be discussed later, lies are intended to get a person something they want or avoid something they don't want (i.e. keep them out of trouble).

3) Lies are intended to deceive. A lie is crafted, not made up, as is bullshit. It is likely that liars have more respect for the intelligence of the people that are lied to since the lie has to be somewhat believable.

4) Bullshitters, because they make things up to fit whatever "sale" of information or product obtains at the time, probably have less respect for the intelligence of the audience. They are selling by throwing ideas against the wall... whatever sticks, sticks.

5) Whether a lie is believed or not depends on the reputation and believability of the liar, whether the lie is reasonable/possible, and the gullibility, knowledge/ignorance and intelligence of the audience. Plus whether the listener *wants* to believe the bullshit, as would be the case if you need a savior who will promise jobs and/or better economic times.

6) There is another difference between lies and bullshit... the units by which they are measured. Lies

are counted by packs or bunches, as in, "That's a pack (or bunch) of lies!" Bullshit is measured in piles or loads, as in, "That's a pile (or load) of bullshit!"

7) Which brings us to the topic of "fake news." When President Trump invokes "fake news" in one of his tweets, it is obvious that he disagrees with whatever claim he calls "fake," and therefore his claim does not reference the truth, but rather is only an attempt to convince an audience of the story he is selling. It is an all-around, vague response to anything disagreed with. Thus, whenever "fake news" is invoked, it is clearly and undoubtedly an example of BULLSHIT!

There are complicating factors, however. Dr. Frankfurt's definition only addresses bullshit *at the original source*. Once the bullshit or lie is out of the bag (or barn, choose your metaphor), and has spread quickly through the populace, is it a lie or is it bullshit? Did the secondary perpetrator, who might also be called a "repeater," know the truth and seek to hide it, or did he speak to influence others and may not even know or care what is truth and what is fiction? That's the first question.

Many of us will reply, "Bullshit!" to something we see as untruthful, without knowing whether what we heard was a lie, or bullshit, or both. Remember, if it is bullshit then it is a lie, but if it's a lie it's not necessarily bullshit in the sense of being made up to fit the situation. So as an expletive, crying "Bullshit!" is the Swiss Army knife of disbelief.

Dictionaries define bullshit as "nonsense, lies, or exaggeration,"[10] "foolish or untrue words or ideas,"[11] and "foolish insolent talk."[12] Notice that in both the proverb above and Brandolini's asymmetry principle, lies can be substituted for bullshit and bullshit for lies. If you think about it, bullshit involves speech that is made up to suit the speaker's purposes, but if a listener spreads the bullshit around, that person is lying, whether he knows it or not. If you need examples, reference President Trump's sycophants, such as Sarah Huckabee Sanders, Kelly Anne Conway, Donald Trump Jr., and a fair percentage of his cabinet secretaries.

The liar and the bullshitter are both stating untruths. Lying and bullshitting are easier to distinguish at the source; after the word has been spread, it's quite difficult to separate them. In fact, many repeaters don't know if they are bullshitting or lying and, in fact, may be accused of both. That's okay, they probably don't care.

For the purposes of our essays, we will sometimes distinguish between lies and bullshit, and at

[10] dictionary.com

[11] learnersdictionary.com

[12] Merriam-Webster.com

other times put them in the same category. The goal is to help the reader distinguish the truth or falsity of the information being pushed at them, without regard to the motivation or awareness of the liar or bullshitter.

2: WHAT TURNED ME ON TO FILTERING BULLSHIT

I, as were most of the youngsters of my generation, was schooled in the honesty, decency and ethicality of our country's leaders. Remember little George Washington?

"When George... ...was about six years old, he was made the wealthy master of a hatchet, of which, like most little boys, he was immoderately fond, and was constantly going about chopping every thing that came in his way. One day, in the garden, where he often amused himself hacking his mother's pea-sticks, he unluckily tried the edge of his hatchet on the body of a beautiful young English cherry-tree, which he barked so terribly, that I don't believe the tree ever got the better of it. The next morning the old gentleman finding out what had befallen his tree, which, by the by, was a great favourite, came into the house, and with much warmth asked for the mischievous author, declaring at the same time, that he would not have taken five guineas for his tree. Nobody could tell him any thing about it. Presently George and his hatchet made their appearance. George, said his father, do you know who killed that beautiful little cherry-tree yonder in the garden? This was a tough question; and George staggered under it for a moment; but quickly recovered himself: and looking at his father, with the sweet face of youth brightened with the inexpressible charm of all-conquering truth, he bravely cried out, 'I can't tell a lie, Pa; you know I can't tell a lie. I did cut it with my hatchet.'–Run to my arms, you dearest boy, cried his father in transports, run to my arms; glad am I, George, that you killed my tree; for you have paid me for it a thousand fold. Such an act of heroism in my son, is more worth than a thousand trees, though blossomed with silver, and their fruits of purest gold."[13]

And then there was Honest Abe and F.D.R. who saw us through a World War and got us out of the Great Depression. For me, the awakening

---

[13] Weems, Mason Locke. "The Fable of George Washington and the Cherry Tree." From <u>The Life of George Washington</u>, 1809.

came around the year 2000, with the election of George W. Bush.

What follows is a story written in a few years ago. It is a tale of the winding road taken by a boy who started out as an innocent and trusting lad to a student of obfuscation, dissembling, equivocating and prevarication, not to mention an avid consumer of bullshit avoidance techniques.

It's the middle of April, 2015. It seemed like a long slog since the end of the football season, but finally baseball has arrived. I'm not a crazy fan. I enjoy the journey. My favorite team is the Yankees, but my backup is the Mets. This year the Yankees (as of April 15, 2015) seem doomed to suck eggs, so I've switched my full-throated allegiance to the Mets, much to the amusement of my friends who, as died-in-the-wool Met fans, have suffered silently for many years. Scratch the "silently." My goal as a fan is to be entertained for the entire six month regular season. If a team that I like is competitive through September, I'm happy. It keeps my head "in the game." Or on it. I can enjoy checking the scores and watching the games occasionally. If they're still around for the playoffs in October, it's a bonus. I understand I'm unusual in this regard; some of my friends who are Met fans cannot say the word "Yankees" without scowling, but that's not how I'm wired.

Baseball or football fandom is relatively simple. You root for your team, occasionally dislike one or two others (such as the Red Sox for a Yankee fan, the Dallas Cowboys for a N.Y. Giants fan), but you don't *hate* them. The feeling is best defined as "grudging respect" for opponents that outplay your proteges. But it seems that just as the new baseball season is beginning, so is the 2016 Presidential race. Primary candidates are beginning to come out of the woodwork. And politics, like baseball, is also a game, but a much more serious one. Politics is less black and white and more red and blue. Perhaps "black and blue" fits best.

Taking sides in a political contest is obviously a more consequential endeavor than rooting for a favorite team, at least when added up over millions of Americans. If your team loses a critical game or series one is usually over it by the next day. If the jerk in the other party beats your guy in a Presidential race you are reminded of it, day after day, for four years. Grudging respect can give way to dislike and disdain, since the result of an election can determine the kind of world your kids grow up in, what's left in your bank account after you've paid taxes, and whether or not we're at war.

For the first 50 or so years of my life I wasn't overly tuned into politics. I voted, usually for a Democrat, but not always. I paid only cursory attention to newspapers and occasionally listened to the news on radio or TV, and I don't recall having vehement feelings about many issues. That changed in 2000.

I followed much of the Iran-Contra hearings in the late 1980s and was very impressed by the reasoning of, and questions asked by, Senator Al Gore from Tennessee. When he ran for President in 2000, I was firmly in the tank for him[14]. I remember watching the Presidential debates with George W. Bush and thinking that Gore ran circles around his opponent in

---

[14] Wasn't there a song, "I Got Algorhyhm"???

terms of substance and the intelligence he radiated. I overlooked, or conveniently ignored, his wooden delivery, his condescension and his arrogance. Hey, you can't have everything.

We all know how the story turned out. I felt that the election was stolen, intentionally or not, by a confluence of factors, including the intercession of the Secretary of State of Florida, Kathleen Harris, and a questionable decision by the Supreme Court. Gore won the popular vote by half a million and good old Ralph Nader, who could've dropped out of the race before the election, got 3% of the vote, most of which came at the expense of Gore. Though I thought highly of Nader before that election, I lost all respect for him as a result of his non-action. So much for taking one for the team.

From then on I became, if not a political "junkie," a "frequent abuser." I remember that within six months of the inauguration, I collected Times headlines in which someone in the Bush administration had pissed off another world leader, country or peoples, typified by Donald Rumsfeld's "old Europe" comment.

Interrupting the story briefly, a recent article, on voter suppression reminded me of some to the gory details of the 2000 theft. "[Republicans knew] the importance of controlling the machinery that decided the rules for voting, the conditions upon which those votes would be cast, and whose vote counted and whose did not. In 2000, the Florida secretary of state, Katherine Harris, proved this point beyond all doubt. Ms. Harris, a delegate at the Republican National Convention that year and a co-chairwoman of George W. Bush's Florida campaign, used her power to undermine the recount. ...She had the full support of the presidential candidate's brother, Gov. Jeb Bush, who surreptitiously sent in his fixer, the Republican lobbyist Mac Stipanovich, to keep the secretary of state focused."[15]

Since the Republicans controlled the rules by which votes were counted, the fix was in, and Bush eked out a victory in Florida which gave him the Presidency. Back to the story...

Following the news through both of W's administrations, I really came to dislike the man or, to be more accurate, the policies,

---

[15] Anderson, Carol. "The Republican Approach to Voter Fraud: Lie." New York Times Op-Ed, 9/8/18.

that he represented. I knew he was a nice guy and all that rot, but from the non-plussed look on his face when he was told of 9-11, to the bad decisions he made throughout his tenure which involved (looking from the outside) giving way too much responsibility and deference to his hawkish underlings Rumsfeld and Cheney, which had the eventual effect of destabiliz-ing the entire Middle East, to his braggado-cio ("mission accomplished") and poor judgment ("Brownie, you're doing a heck of a job" [on Hurricane Katrina]), this was a boy in a man's job. He was way out of his league. The only major stance that Bush ever took that I supported was his stance on a pathway to citizenship for immigrants.

By the time the 2008 election rolled around, I would've voted for a gerbil over the Republican nominee.[16] I favored Oba-ma, but would have been satisfied had Clinton won the nomination. In a way, I had reverse prejudice; I wanted Obama to win, just because he was black, though I had had good feelings about him since

---

[16] Which, whether I like it or not, helps me understand why people would vote for a gerbil before Hillary Clinton.

2005, when I heard him take a joke and give a few on the NPR weekly quiz show, "Wait, Wait, Don't Tell Me!" He was quick witted, humble and seemed a "regular guy." He also seemed honest, for a politician at least.

I admired John McCain, but thought that Obama danced all over and around him in the debates and loved to hate the travesty that was Sarah Palin. I remember the schadenfreude of watching her self-destruct in front of the whole nation. McCain didn't deserve that humiliation, but he either picked her out of desperation because he was way behind in the polls or, at minimum, allowed her to be selected by the party hacks. She was a great package but was hollow inside.

I voted early in 2008, getting to the polling place at the local middle school about 15 minutes before it opened, so as not to be late for work. I was about sixth in line, behind five African-Americans. I was proud to be an American that day, and for some time thereafter. Having lived through the Martin Luther King era and the race riots of the late 1960s, it was and is still heart-warming to me that our country, for all its faults, had the balls to elect an African-American.

Through the six and a half years of his Presidency, I've been his defender most of the time, though I think he squandered the 60 vote majority in the Senate that he briefly enjoyed. I also think he could have been more forceful; not necessarily in foreign policy, for that is a morass in which every path has negative unintended consequences, but here at home with the likes of McConnell and Boehner.

When he ran for re-election in 2012, I still thought he was on the right side of most issues. For example, I believe that abortion should be a woman's choice, that the government was right in bailing out GM and large private financial institutions, that we should stop financing the oil industry, that the Citizen's United decision was a total disaster (understatement), that we shouldn't need a photo ID in order to vote, that we should support the development of alternate energy sources, that humans contribute to climate change, that we need more regulation of guns, that the Affordable Care Act was good for the country, that we should work towards a humane immigration policy, that there should be an independent Palestinian state, that gay marriage should be legal, that evolution is real, that the Constitution and Bill of Rights need to be updated and that the wealthy should pay more taxes than they do currently. Mitt Romney, the Republican nominee, was on the other side of almost every one of the above issues.[17]

Political leanings aside, I believe that we all need to approach political contests with more than a measure of caution and a heap of discernment. Technology moves so fast that our ability to understand and deal with its ramifications always seems to be a step behind. In the same manner, the expansion of political tactics and strategies have left us open to a host of effects that have left us in a pickle. The increased injection of money into politics may have the same effect as the universal availability of technology to bad actors. In a way, there's not much difference between the wealthy being able to influence elections and

---

[17] Issues selected from the 75 presented at http://2012election.pro-con.org/view.source-summary-chart.php

would-be terrorists being able to influence millions of innocents over the internet. The analogy is not exact, but it's close. We trust people with money or global access to act well. Most do, some don't.

The story above was written in 2015, before Donald Trump announced that he was running for President. What emerges from it is, that political differences aside, the limitless reach provided by the internet and the power of unimaginable amounts of money into the social and political arena, laid the groundwork for the current EOB (Era of Bullshit) which includes, but is not limited to, the ascendancy of Donald J. Trump. In other words, it is technology and filthy lucre that have allowed the explosion of lies and bullshit.

The same 2000 election that turned me on to politics, helped to insinuate lying into the national ethos. "The final and perhaps most important lesson from 2000 was to lie. Lie often. Say the lies loud; say them with pride. Lie over and over and over. Lie without shame. Lie until the truth is drowned out, dead. Lie until no amount of evidence could convince anyone otherwise. Lie until there is no other narrative."[18]

---

[18] Anderson, Carol. op. cit.

So here in 2018, with the midterm elections around the corner and the 2020 presidential election looming, we need to become more educated consumers of information. Let's face it, we are all ignorant by degrees of what's really going on in our country and the world. We're not stupid, but we have limited time and energy to fact-check or even digest everything that's thrown at us. What follows are things to look for and be aware of, when heaps of disparate information is pushed at us. Put another way, we need to able to separate the wheat from the chaff. The more lies and bullshit pervade our society, the more and better tools we need to fight them.

3: WHO BULLSHITS AND LIES?

The short answer is that we all do, by degrees. Do any of the following sound familiar?:

I didn't know I was going that fast, Officer.

I had a great time last night. I'll call you soon.

The dog ate my homework, Mrs. Flembroke.

Do you like this shirt? I got it on sale on sale for $12!

Sorry I'm late. Got stuck in traffic.

Let's see… I had a six on that hole.

I just mailed that check.

We all lie. Well, maybe Mother Teresa didn't cheat at golf. Notice that all of these "explanations" have one thing in common; to protect a person from a penalty or criticism or embarrassment. The protective quality of lying will be revisited later.

But there's another overarching source of bull-shit: people who use it to get something they want:

That dress is definitely you!

This ten year old car is a beaut! It'll go another 100,000 miles.

Of course I love you!

Vote for Tweakford. He'll bring our jobs back.

This stock is a can't-miss.

If you stray from the flock, you'll go straight to
hell!

The commonality among the above examples is
that you have something that someone else wants,
and they will say whatever they have to say to get it
from you. Notice that while the first group of statements were lies, they were not necessarily bullshit.
This second group is bullshit, because the truth is of
no interest to the bullshitter. For them, the ends justifies the means. Often it's your money that they covet,
at other times it's your beliefs, or your sex or your
presence at a place of worship. They realize that this is
something you might not otherwise do on your own,
so you have to be sold on it.

Does the bullshitter know they are lying or are
they oblivious? When used to protect (from penalty,
criticism or embarrassment), the liar is almost surely
aware that they are hiding the truth. When used by
someone to get something from you, it's not always
clear.

Take the situation a car salesman finds himself
in. Upon being hired, he is probably schooled in the

specs and advantages of the brand of vehicle he is selling (engineering, style, price, snob appeal), as well as the nuances of salesmanship. Does he lie to customers? Probably, but not all the time and after a while he is not conscious of doing so. So as not to think of himself as a congenital liar, he will develop rationalizations such as a) his brand is better than the others or at least as good, b) if he doesn't talk that couple into buying, some other schmo will, c) he has to put food on the table for his family.

Do politicians bullshit? Almost all do, but there are degrees. Some will say that the ends justify the means so that anything that they need to say to help them get elected is fair game. If they believe in their cause they might sacrifice verity for what they deem a higher truth. And, after all, it's survival of the fittest and their career and livelihood is at stake. (In this way, they are very similar to car salesmen.) Some will believe all or most of what they say and whether it really is the whole truth, partial truth or total baloney is irrelevant, especially after the fiftieth time they've said the same thing. Some will know when they fabricate but might think and/or say that their opponent is worse and lies more than they.

Other professions also shade the truth, with similar motivations. Members of the extreme left and right media try to sway the opinions of their audiences to their side and/or reflect the views of their followers, thus maintaining the existing echo chambers (which may contain varying degrees of the truth).[19]

Members of the clergy may offer carrots and sticks, in the form of heaven and hell to their flocks, so as to ensure their continued employment. While this may sound cynical, the clergy are not just selling a belief in God, they are selling *their* particular brand of God. In this way, they are also similar to car salesmen, but probably have a better product to offer.

Although all of us bullshit and/or lie anywhere from a little to a lot, the consequences of those lies need to be taken into account. If I lie to protect myself by saying, "Sorry I'm late. I hit traffic," I'm only lying to one or several people. If I lie by saying, "There was no collusion" or "There was no obstruction of justice," so as to escape censure by the Congress or the Judiciary, there are consequences that may affect all Americans through a possible Constitutional crisis down the road. So one dimension to be considered is the significance of the falsehood, based on the number of people affected and the severity of the effect on those people.

Another dimension is whether the liar suspects,

---

[19] Just one of a myriad of examples: Right in the middle of Hurricane Florence's attack on the southeast, Paul Manafort, Trump's one-time campaign manager, signed a plea agreement with Bob Mueller. This was a big deal. I have news apps on my phone, and CNN featured the hurricane story first and Manafort's flip second. FOX news also led with the hurricane, but the Manafort saga was consigned to around tenth in importance.

knows or has no inkling of the falsehood. Some politicians suspect they are not telling the truth, or at least distorting it, but do so for what they consider a higher purpose. The purpose may vary as well; to fulfill an idealistic goal, or self-serve by getting re-elected and ensuring their own survival. The ones that know they are lying somehow seem more evil than those that don't, and the ones that lie merely to ensure survival seem worse than those who do it for idealistic reasons. Those that lie without knowing it, by repeating something they've heard, can be called "cattle," or ignorant, or can be accused of having "drunk the Kool-aid."

One more category of lies is called "lying by omission." This can be just as innocent or destructive as regular lies or bullshit. If I don't tell Sally that I think her dress is ugly, I am lying by omission, but do so with a higher motive; to spare Sally's feelings. (Even if she asks me if I like the dress and I lie by saying, "It's very nice," I am "fibbing" or telling a "white lie" with the same purpose in mind.) However, as a candidate for political office, if I purposely "forget" to report that I have a DUI on my record and was arrested for drug possession earlier in my life, or have had a dozen contacts with Russian businessmen over the last few years, the sin is a lot greater.

4: WHO ARE THE VICTIMS OF BULLSHIT?

Again, the short answer is we all are, by degrees. There are various categories of victims, however. The first group are the people that hear the bullshit directly. Suppose a political candidate or operative invokes a conspiracy theory and broadcasts, over media friendly to his cause, that the opposing candidate is involved in some kind of conspiracy, such as "the Deep State."[20]

People who hear about this "conspiracy" from Breitbart don't question it; *they want it to be true because it fits right in with the other beliefs that they hold*. If it didn't fit their belief system, they wouldn't be reading Breitbart. The Deep State theory fits smoothly into their individual echo chambers, which seeks consistent data and ignores or rejects dissonant data.[21] Even willing consumers of bullshit may be unwitting victims.

A second group of victims are what can be called "the repeaters" who, in effect, just go along for

---

[20] The Deep State theory invokes the existence of a group of elitists within the government to control and manipulate policies of the government. Recent promoters of this theory include alt-right media including Breitbart and Info Wars. Source: wikipedia.

[21] Gribin, Anthony. I Am An Echo Chamber: The Basis of Tribalism. ttgPress, 2018.

the ride. They don't do much reading themselves, aren't tuned in to network television news, and are generally cynical about politics and politicians. They hear about news in the break room at work, from a guy in their carpool, from an overheard conversation at a backyard barbecue or from a family member. These folks aren't in the tank for any particular candidate or policy but, not wanting to appear ignorant, glom onto whatever they hear and make it part of their own echo chamber. While the first group won't question the existence of the Deep State because they want to believe in it, the repeaters won't question it because they really don't know enough to be familiar with any counterarguments. If someone only hears one side of an issue, they are not likely to disagree.

One hope for this second group to see bullshit in any conspiracy theory is for them to learn how to do due diligence. In other words, they'll have to do some reading on their own. As we all know, however, this is highly unlikely. Another hope is that public figures from sports and movie stars to scientists to elected officials speak the truth and condemn bullshit whenever they see or hear it. The problem with speaking out, however, is that it might hurt your career. Just ask Colin Kaepernick. It is especially true in the political realm, since speaking out might get you "primaried" if the powers that be see you as a traitor.

An example of this is that despite overwhelming evidence of global climate change, many politicians, mostly conservatives, will not validate the need to address global warming. Why? Because it goes against many Republicans' and President Trump's pro-fossil fuel policies (including hiring and supporting the ex-Secretary of the Environmental Protection Agency, Scott Pruitt who doggedly attempted to cripple environmental protection). They fear being attacked by the President or challenged by right wingers in their party, and voted out of office.

A third hope for the repeaters is to *question the motivation* of the source. When a person hears something that may or may not be true, ask yourself, "What's in it for them?" "How do they benefit from what they just said?" "What are they trying to get me to do?" This type of questioning is a lot easier than asking people to do their own due diligence, and is therefore more likely to work. What will become clear to the cynic is that *self-interest lies behind almost every instance of lying and bullshitting*. More on this in the next chapter.

5: WHY DO WE BULLSHIT AND LIE?

We are all taught, "honesty is the best policy." Many famous people have addressed this issue. Thomas Jefferson said, "Honesty is the first chapter in the book of wisdom." William Shakespeare believed, "No legacy is so rich as honesty." And Donald Trump declared, "I judge people based on their capability, honesty, and merit."[22]

Then again, Mark Twain quipped, saying, "Honesty is the best policy - when there is money in it."[23] Groucho Marx' thoughts were along the same line, "The secret of life is honesty and fair dealing. If you can fake that, you've got it made."[24] Twain and Marx, in an amusing way, point to the answer to the question of why we bullshit and lie. There's got to be something in it for us.

The sad but true answer is that we bullshit and lie if and when it is in our self-interest. Not to say we lie all the time, but when we do, we are either protecting ourselves from an unwanted consequence or are trying to get something we want. In the last chapter, it

---

[22] The irony of this quote, coming from this famous person, will not be lost on the alert reader.

[23] All quotes above taken from brainyquote.com @https://www.brainyquote.com/search_results?q=honesty

[24] ibid.

was shown that people will lie to avoid a) a penalty, as in avoiding a speeding ticket or after-school detention, b) criticism, for spending too much money on a shirt or being reamed out for being late to a meeting, or c) embarrassment, after shooting a twelve on a par 3, or for not wanting to ask someone out on a second date.

Alternately, we might lie to get something we want. We might want to sell someone on a car, or a stock, or talk them into inviting us up to their apartment after a date. Or to continue attending church or to vote for a candidate that we don't support or against a candidate that we do.

Self-interest can be divided into two main categories: protective and direct. Protective self-interest (PSI) motivates us to lie to protect ourselves from consequences, criticism or embarrassment. Direct self-interest (DSI) drives us to try to get what we want. A full discussion of self-interest can be found in the book Selfonomics, by this author.[25]

In order to steel ourselves against bullshit and lies, we need to examine the "whys" of that behavior. We need to ask ourselves questions such as, "How does she benefit from that statement?" What will he get if I buy what he wants me to buy? What is in *his* self-interest? Two examples involve getting a new car

[25] Gribin, Anthony J. Selfonomics: How Broadly Defined Self-Interest Explains Everything. ttgPress, 2013.

and investing your money. Each dealership and each salesperson within each dealership are out to make as much money as possible. So they will try to "sell up," meaning get you to buy a more expensive car, to add as many options as possible for that car, to use the dealership's own finance team for the loan on your car, to buy an extended warranty and even get you to lease instead of buy (since in effect they sell the car twice; to you and the second buyer). Why do they do these things? To make you happy? No. Each of these choices will make the salesperson and the dealership more money.

Investing is even more complicated. Most legitimate brokers are obligated to obey or voluntarily adhere to the "fiduciary rule," or "the simple premise that when giving advice with regard to retirement funds — brokers, investment advisers, and insurance agents must act in the best interests of their clients. Before the rule, brokers had only to ensure their recommendations were 'suitable,' a lower standard."[26] If they don't or won't, you shouldn't be doing business with them.

For instance, if you want to purchase mutual funds, how much commission are you paying to the fund and your broker? The difference between funds

---

[26] Munnell, Alicia H. "Fiduciary rule takes a hit in the Fifth Circuit." marketwatch, 4/12/18.

that charge 1% per year and funds that charge .5% per year will be enormous when compounded over many years. Exchange traded funds (ETFs) charge even less. Does the broker make more money if you buy propri- etary funds (i.e. funds sponsored by his own broker- age firm) than if you go with another company's fund family? Each time you make a trade, buying or selling a stock, how much do you pay in fees? These are all issues that are difficult to address, especially because the broker has a lot more information and knowledge about stocks and bonds than you do, but if you don't address them, you'll probably come out on the short end of the stick.

The buyer is generally in less trouble with the car salesman, because with a little research on the in- ternet and a willingness to shop at several dealerships to negotiate the price, you buyer should get close to the best deal possible. With investment advisors, it's tough to shop around, and once you've parked your money somewhere, it's difficult to move it because an investor usually has a relationship with their advisor. But with investments, one can lose thousands, as compared to a car decision, which might only cost you a few hundred.

People who lie to protect themselves, often have innocent reasons. If I tell a young lady that I will call her after a first date, while having absolutely no inten- tion of so doing, what is my motivation for dissembling? I could say, "I'm just not feelin' it, Barbara, but it was nice meeting you." Or, "You're very nice Barbara, but I'm not attracted to you." Or, "I don't think we should go out again. It's me, not you." Or, being the chicken that I am, I can say, "I'll give you a call next week." Easy peasy, especially since we don't live near each other and I'll never have to see her again. Saves me from an uncomfortable conversation and helps me avoid hurting another person. And since Barbara, who is probably not stupid, can tell from my behavior that I'm not dropping another dime[27] to ask her out, can save face by seeing me as a liar for saying I'll call (and then don't), and/or can tell her girlfriends that I was a dog or not very nice.

Or suppose I lie to my parents about my homework or grades. They ask me how I'm doing and I say, "Fine," preferring to omit reporting that 43 on a math test. Or if asked about my English homework, I say, "Sure...I did it in school," though I was more interested in talking to the hottie sitting next to me in that class. Instead of trying to avoid embarrassment, my lies are designed to save my ass from some kind of punishment which might involve grounding or loss of phone, which is my lifeline to the world outside of home. Kids who are caught early in these types of lies

---

[27] For you younger readers, "dropping a dime" means making a phone call.

and are suitably punished tend not to recidivate, but those whose lies are scolded but not punished will continue to use prevarication as a method, however misguided, of enjoying life. They get to know that they only have to face the music once at the end of each marking period at report card time which, since they only get lectured, is definitely worth it. (At least until they have to apply to college.)

Of course, protective lying can be a lot less inno-cent than the above dating and homework situations. Ones that have can possibly have enormous effects on the lives of individuals, such as a husband repeatedly cheating and denying it, or a politician making promises that, when they aren't fulfilled, hurt the lives of many people.

6: WHO ARE MOST SUSCEPTIBLE TO BULLSHIT AND LIES?

All of us, at one time or another, have been in a situation where people are talking about something about which we have little or no knowledge. This may occur at a neighborhood barbecue, at work, or a family gathering. What is going on inside our heads when this happens? And as you go through the following three situations, which of the people do you think are most susceptible to falling for bullshit and/or lies?

First situation: Three guys are sitting around talking (bullshitting in the *good* sense of the word) about baseball in depth, including teams you don't like and players that you don't know. It may get a little boring after a while, but because you love the sport of soccer, you can understand their love of baseball, and don't think less of the people in that conversation. You can sit there and let them bullshit without feeling threatened by their knowledge, and without needing to put them down in your own mind. Whatever floats their boat...yer picks yer poison... each to his own...

Second situation: You are well-educated and in a white collar career, such as manager in a big corporation, and you are sitting around listening to three guys in blue collar occupations talking about home repair projects in which they are involved. The extent of your own handiness only extends to changing light bulbs and calling in people to fix whatever breaks. When you were young the tools in your house consisted of one screwdriver, one hammer and one wrench. You feel slightly inadequate and a tad jealous of their abilities, and you listen intently, occasionally throwing in "wows" to complement their achievements. You don't feel too bad about yourself, however, because you can fall back on the knowledge that you went to college (and they probably didn't) and don't have to get dirty to earn a living. You would never throw your white collar career up to them as superior, first because it would be impolite, second because they're nice guys, and third because you're outnumbered and they have big muscles. So a summation of how you feel is slightly envious of their skills and slightly superior to them in terms of your place on the status ladder.

Third situation: You are a high school graduate in a blue collar career, such as plumbing, and you are sitting around listening to three guys in white collar occupations talking about immigration or the economy. You don't have much knowledge about what they are discussing, but their views are clearly liberal and are hostile to President Trump. They don't exclude you from the conversation, but don't exactly include you either, so you feel ignored and left out.

They use high fallutin' language and are dismissive of anyone who disagrees with them. You are sure that they look down on people who support the President, including you. They don't accuse you of anything, but you are sure they know that you are on the "other side." Because you know very little about the subject under discussion, you don't want to get into it because you'll probably look and feel foolish. You're pretty sure they think of you as stupid and uneducated.

Feeling looked down upon is not a pleasant feeling. You can either beat yourself up for not being interested in school and not going to college or you can sit there in angry silence. If you are the type that beats himself up, you are likely to always avoid these types of discussions because it only results in self-flagellation.

If you don't tend to beat yourself up, you will turn your emotions outward and feel anger towards those *fucking intellectual snobs*. They think they're better than everyone else because they have an education. You sit listening to them talk for a while, saying nothing because you are outgunned and outnumbered, at least until your heightened blood pressure insists that you excuse yourself. You vow to never get into this kind of situation again. When your wife suggests that you get together with these same people in a few months, you tell her you can't stand several of those guys, because they think they're better than us. You're not gonna play.

What's going on here? As a psychologist, I can tell you that this third situation began way before our plumber even thought of being a plumber. It started in primary school. Boys tend to know who the good athletes, strong kids and smart ones are in their grade school classes. Girls have an equivalent status ladder. As they grow up they are "tracked" by how well they do in school. There are "'tard" classes, average classes and accelerated classes, but early on most kids are oblivious to this as they move through the grades with the same kids.

By high school, the "die is cast." You were pigeonholed as a popular kid, and/or a jock, or a preppy, a band/drama kid, a gearhead, a druggie, in special ed, a brain in advanced classes, or just an average kid with a few friends but no allegiance to any group. The nerds and some of the others were college-bound, the rest comfortable with going to a community college or finding a job.

The status ladder, which usually had the popular kids and athletes at the top, and the nerds at the bottom, reversed after high school. The nerds went to good colleges and started careers in a profession or in the financial sector. The middle-of-the-road students went to community colleges and also found ways to make a living. The ones who quit after high school went into jobs, rather than careers. Some eventually found their way into the trades, in which they could make decent living by working hard.

Many kids who were not college bound knew for years that school was not for them. They struggled to keep up in the three R's early in the early grades, either because they had trouble paying attention or just couldn't grasp things as quickly or well as the smart kids. Some may have had behavioral problems and developed reputations by the beginning of middle school. After a series of failures, many of them stopped trying to succeed, often "forgot" homework or fudged their way through it. In class, their thoughts were elsewhere, since once you fall behind it's very difficult to catch up. Especially if you have no interest in doing so.

The kids that turned off to school early on were likely to not have intellectual interests as adults. They read little aside from magazines or sports sections, don't follow current events closely and have little interest in the arts or sciences. Some may regret the path not taken, but realize that they were trapped in the directions they chose, consciously or unconsciously, a long time ago.

So what happens when they are in the presence of, or are lectured by, those intellectual snobs? They avoid them and the information they are pushing in silence until… a champion appears. A champion that speaks their language and tells them that they are the real Americans, and that those bicoastal elites aren't going to run their lives any more. This person promises to bring their jobs back, to put more money in their paychecks with tax cuts, to stop immigrants from taking their jobs and raping and pillaging, to stop other countries from taking us to the cleaners, to stop minorities from milking the system.

Enter Donald Trump, who offered a reprieve from a lifelong inferiority complex. Who tells them that they don't have to suffer in silence any more. That they can give voice to the deeply seated resentments that they've harbored most of their lives. Does anyone think that they will abandon their allegiance to him for a trifle? These are the people who are most likely to fall for bullshit and lies; for whom bullshit will be most effective. Mr. Trump was born to fulfill their needs… Hillary Clinton used the word "deplorables" to describe many of these people, which certainly contributed to her loss in the election. A more appropriate phrase might have been "the less educated, less wealthy, less tech savvy, blue collar non-coastals." This would certainly not gone over better with voters, but it would have been more accurate.

7: WHO IS WORSE, A BULLSHITTER OR A LIAR?

"On Father's Day last week, the highest-paid employee of Washington State University tweeted out a video of a 2014 speech by Barack Obama that was altered to make him sound like a one-world-government tyrant.

When called on the fraud, Mike Leach, the head football coach and $3.5 million a year representative of the same school that gave us the legendary newsman Edward R. Murrow, said, "Prove it."

It was easily proven as doctored. But instead of apologizing, and owning up to his dissemination of a fake conspiracy video, he then wrote, "What is a fact?" Of all the things President Trump has done to destroy civil norms, his debasement of language is the most chilling and poisonous. For it has now reached down to every level, allowing people who are supposed to be societal pillars, or even role models, to act as if reality has no foundation."[28]

---

[28] Egan, Timothy. "Trickle Down Trumpsters and the Debasement of Language." New York Times Op-Ed, 6/22/18.

To answer this question we need to dive down deep into the bullshit. Suppose your brother-in-law Jerry tells you that he caught a 23 foot trout in the local stream. You are suitably impressed and ask him if you might see it. He says, "You know, I had on my waders and couldn't reach my cell phone to take a picture while holding the fish in one hand and the pole in the other, so I just released him. What a majestic fish!" Now, you love your sister, but momma didn't raise no fool and you've heard Jerry's fables before, so you just shake your head or roll your eyes or laugh, rather than confronting him. How does your sister live with him? Bless her heart!

Your other sister married Oliver, a guy who loves to tell you about every restaurant that he's eaten in and every trip that he's taken. And, of course, every last one was the absolute best. You hear about the most exquisite Veal Parm on the east coast at Villa Roma and the cutest little village in France that had the best Bordeaux he's ever tasted, a 2011 Grand Cru.

Two things occur to you. One, that your sisters have remarkably terrible taste in men. And two, that you rarely take anything either one of your brother-in-laws say seriously. Very little harm is caused by that type of bullshit. The worst level it ever reaches is that of minor annoyance.

Aside from braggarts, a second category of bull-shitters contains all types of salesman who have a product to sell you. If you are told that the 2018 Phlegmobile is the best car on the road by far, or that you will get an unbelievable price only if you buy it today, most of us won't fall for the sales pitch. Even when the sales manager, the "closer," saunters out to greet you and comes off like your best friend. In fact most of us expect the "hard sell" and can steel ourselves for a trip to the dealership. The hard sell is the reason many people won't shop for a car alone, and why car salesmen are about as popular as dentists and the IRS.

Another subtle type of bullshit is offered by people who do home repairs. As an example, we recently heard some noise in our attic and made some calls to services that remove vermin. We got estimates that ranged from around $1700 to over $14,000. Each of the people were certain they knew what was causing the problem (which ranged from an infestation of baby mice to flying squirrels) (yes, flying squirrels), and were sure they could remediate it. Since neither me not my wife was going to venture into the attic and we are not terminologists, we were kind of at a disadvantage. Sort of like baby mice in the woods.

aOne of the lessons here is to never live in a reasonably good neighborhood. I'd bet the level of bull-shit for home repairs (including plumbers, electricians, etc.) is directly correlated with the price of the house. And the price of car repairs will vary with the value of the car. But as reprehensible as it is for people to try to separate you from your money, when people bullshit to change your beliefs or get you to vote for them, the consequences can be a lot more serious on a large scale.

The reason the belief-sellers are dangerous is that unlike salesmen or bragging brothers-in-law, these people are subtle. The hard sell isn't obvious and often we *want* to believe them because they promise that our lives will be, somehow, better. The bullshitters who can do serious damage to your life, your family's prospects and your country are the ones with wealth and/or power, which tend to run together. Wealth gives you power and power makes it easier to accrue wealth.

Three examples of this category of bullshit artist are Bernie Madoff, Sir Allen Stanford and our president, Donald J. Trump. Madoff ran a Ponzi scheme that bilked investors out of roughly 65 billion dollars. Stanford was sort of a mini-Madoff (only 7 billion stolen), who ran a Ponzi scheme that landed him a 110 year jail sentence. He got off light, since Madoff racked up 150 years behind bars. Which brings us to

Donald Trump, whose bullshitting is a lot more familiar to most Americans.[29]

A psychologist by the name of Stanton Peele devised a cookbook for wannabe bullshitters. What follows is his path to being a master bullshitter in five easy steps.[30]

1. Always remember - people are afraid to challenge you. Both because it violates social propriety, and because of their fears that their own secrets will be found out, people don't question others to their face. So simply count on being allowed to mouth off and make outrageous claims with no fear of being contradicted - or with objectors themselves facing ostracism.

2. Point to your legitimate successes or bona fides. Stanford was a genuine knight (mediated by Antiguan authorities). Madoff had been president of the NASDAQ

---

29 A close friend once quipped, "If Trump weren't rich, he'd be a used car salesman, married to a hooker, living in Las Vegas."

30 Peele, Stanton. "Bullshitting: Lessons from the Masters,How the great bullshitters pull it off." Psychology Today, first posted May 15, 2009. @https://www.psychologytoday.com/us/blog/addiction-in-society/200905/bullshitting-lessons-the-masters

stock exchange's board of directors. There are big buildings with Trump's name gaudily plastered all over them. So simply trot out your past successes (magnified as much as possible) at every opportunity, and add on whatever bullshit you wish.

3. Act arrogant - keep it up. Although arrogance might seem to work against you by offending people, it is the supreme intimidation technique - people are readily cowed when someone acts like he is better, smarter, more powerful than they are. The only danger is if you act modestly or question yourself, because people WILL attack weakness. In fact, even when you are being arrested (as in Stanford's case), attack your accusers.

4. Claim esoteric knowledge or techniques. It doesn't matter if the formula you use to explain your success makes no sense - people aren't secure enough to challenge something they can't understand. In fact, it pays to make the secret to your success as incomprehensible as possible while linking it to something beyond questioning,

like say relativity, quantum physics, evolution or, for the old fashioned, God.

5. Always delay the day of reckoning. Contrary to the idea that, if your are standing on a foundation of bullshit, you will begin to sink, send questioners and doubters away. In the interim, they will become re-intimidated by how highly your bullshit is regarded. When they return (if they have the guts), simply go back to square one, making the same claims with the same evidence, and in the same arrogant, don't-question-me tone."

So the answer to the question as to how much harm can be cause by bullshit: it depends. If it's a personal relationship, how many times does the friend or girlfriend/boyfriend have to lie to you before you never trust anything he or she says? Many people will say just one, unless it's a meaningless one such as "I overslept." Trust is important in a personal relationship but is very fragile, hard to earn, and much harder to earn back. On the other hand, if we know a bullshitter personally, like those aforementioned brothers-in-law, we take them with a grain of salt.

As for salespeople, of all stripes, we expect them to bullshit and lie. The more sophisticated ones may lie by omission, such as not telling you about the difference in commission rates unless you ask, while the less ethical ones will bullshit and lie with abandon; viz. Sir, you need a whole new set of axle-grommets if you don't want your wheels to fall off." The best policy here is to get as many quotes or opinions as possible, check references, and be prepared to lose a few bucks. Hey, it's only money.

The bullshitters that are really dangerous are the ones with wealth and power. The best bullshitters also have a quality that is not on Dr. Steele's list; namely, charisma. To do damage, you have to attract people to your bullshit. Since Donald Trump is foremost an entertainer, that's what he does best. He is (or at least was) good looking, high living, woman attracting, take no prisoners, bullshitting braggart. Note that other wealthy and powerful men, such as the Koch Brothers and George Soros, also bullshit and lie. But they are lacking charisma, so they are not "front men." They use their wealth to influence politics to hire others to bullshit for them through commercials and by backing their chosen candidates.

The problem is that Trump presents the worst of both worlds; he is rich, powerful and charismatic and, is a master bullshitter and liar.[31] These "talents" offer the possibility of ruining the economy (through a tariff war that might sabotage the global economy), changing the values that have made our country great (morality, civility and the welcoming of immigrants), the replacement of democracy with autocracy (due to Trump's narcissism, paranoia and vindictiveness), and eventually revolution (because income inequality, if not addressed, may lead to dire consequences). That's all. Oh, and as the anecdote at the beginning of this chapter implies, he has given license to other role models to ignore truth and facts, in effect creating new horde of bullshitters.

So which is worse, bullshitting or lying? In interpersonal relations, lying is worse. In sales situations, there is more bullshitting than lying, but you can see the bullshit coming. And in the political sphere, it is the combination of the two that can have profound effects on everyone's life.

---

[31] The phrase "pathological liar" may fit, but the definition usually requires that the person lies for no personal gain. It seems that whenever Trump lies, he does so for personal gain, even if it is merely to impress people.

8: WHO OR WHAT GIVES LICENSE TO BULLSHIT?

A definition of "give license to" is "[to give someone] an excuse to behave in an irresponsible or excessive way."[32] Synonyms include permit, entitle and authorize. There is also the connotation of breaking the ice of some social norm. When "All In The Family" aired in 1971, many people were shocked to hear the sound of a toilet flushing on the soundtrack. That alone may have made the show a hit. Compare that with the liberal use of profanity on television today. Once the ice was broken in terms of potty talk (pun intended), it was a slippery slope and very difficult to undo. Other examples can be found in child rearing. Once a parent allows a sleepover or attendance at a concert or turns over the keys to the car, going back is next to impossible.

Will the same be true or the incivility and bad behavior that has taken over American politics recently? Many people were reviled at the way Donald Trump ran his campaign to be the Republican nominee in 2016. He made up disparaging nicknames for almost every serious rival, enabled if not encouraged physical attacks and profanity at his rallies, and bullshitted repeatedly about his beliefs and policies to fit

---

[32] https://www.collinsdictionary.com/us/dictionary/english/license

whatever audience he was currently addressing. His bullshit and outrageous lies came at such a furious rate that much of the population simply became numb to his utterances. He became a role model for anyone who saw political correctness as snobbery, foisted on the masses by the intellectual elite. But he is fairly low down on the list of the licensers of bullshit, even though he is the most visible and vocal current purveyor. He is only the tip of the iceberg.

The first, and probably most important culprit, is the growth of technology over the decades. As was discussed in Chapter 8, we can reach more people at greater distances and with total anonymity. With anonymity comes impunity, so that if we lie to someone or bullshit, making up information about a person or a policy, there are rarely any consequences to be paid. A guy on a dating site can bullshit to a woman, a fundamentalist group can lie to attract vulnerable youth to its cause and a politician can make promises that can never be fulfilled. The liars and bullshitters are not held to account.

A second culprit is self-interest, which is the motivation behind the bullshit. We bullshit to get what we want and to protect ourselves from negative consequences. Self-interest "gooses" the power of technology and technology catalyzes self-interest.

Another licenser of bullshit, similar to technology, is wealth, since wealth also increases the use and reach of bullshit. If wealthy, I can buy more advertising and air time to spread my gospel so as to influence the results of elections. Which brings us to another, non-intuitive factor: the Constitution of the United States of America.

Surprised? Well, consider the year 2010, which was a great year for licensing bullshit. An originalist interpretation of the Constitution[33] resulted in two decisions that allowed unlimited amounts of money into political campaigns. Citizen's United is the most famous of the two, from which "corporations are people" became a laugh line. The SpeechNow decision empowered the formation of "super PACs" (Political Action Committees) which can receive huge sums of cash from any people or organizations. They cannot communicate or coordinate with individual candidates, but they can use their money to support both candidates and issues that they favor ad libitum. And they obviously know which way their candidates would want them to lean, with or without communication.

An interesting thing about super PACs is that they don't have to disclose their donors. The only hint to where the money comes from in the ad itself, aside from the obvious one-sided message, is the name of

---

[33] "Originalism" results in that strict interpretation, as opposed to "Living Constitutionalism," which avers that the meaning of the document changes over time.

the sponsor, as in "This ad was paid for by Restore Our Future." In general, if the name of PAC includes the word "progressive" or "democracy" they lean left, if the name includes "conservative" or "American" they lean right. Not that you couldn't tell by the content of the broadside.

Since the PACs are governed by virtually no rules short of slander, they have the philosophical will and financial incentive to lie, bullshit, exaggerate and distort information either to support their candidate (or issue) or destroy their opponent. Therefore in my opinion, *we should automatically and totally discount any message delivered to us by a PAC.* The only adverts we should pay any attention to are those which are sponsored by a particular candidate, since at least we can hold them responsible for what is said.

Why is this important? Citizen's United and Speech Now were deemed as constitutional under *a strict interpretation* of the document. It is not that our Founding Fathers wanted to bullshit us or had bad intentions or were not intelligent. The problem (silly them!) is they did not and could not, have foreseen the future. They could not have anticipated the advent and reach of telephony, television and the internet, all of which allow contact over great distances. They could not have seen that the document they wrote would allow (and incentivize) the rich to inject their wealth into political races, or would allow the disenfranchisement of millions due to putting roadblocks in the way of voting. They gave us the best wisdom they had at the time, but to them, blacks were slaves. How could they have been expected to deal with voter suppression for a segment of society that wasn't considered a segment of society? The result over a few centuries is that those with wealth and access to technology can lie and bullshit to promote their agendas and most of us are powerless to deal with it.

When the Constitution was written, the purposes of guns was to defend the homeland against invasion. (Even hunting with muskets was an adventure since what emerged from the gun was scattershot.) Armies and militias had armories filled with guns. Today, over a million people, most of whom are gun collectors or enthusiasts have their own personal armories, hopefully locked away in gun safes in their basements or garages. 99.999 percent of those personal armories are owned by responsible gun enthusiast or collectors, but the .001 percent might present a clear and present danger to the population. So when the NRA gives bullshit excuses to counter any attempt at reasonable gun control ("they're coming for our guns," "it's a slippery slope," "guns don't kill people, people do"), it is the Constitution, and the people who espouse originalist interpretations of it, who block any legislation that weakens the Second Amendment.

The same criticism of the Constitution can be weighed against its omission of education as a right of citizenship. To our forefathers, education was an unnecessary luxury for most people. Americans lived in an agrarian society or worked with their hands. Education, aside from a basic ability to read and write, was unnecessary. Today, that's obviously untrue. Anyone who isn't well educated is behind the eight ball. Fortunately, states have taken up the slack and required public education through high school for all students, but there are great disparities among the states in terms of how much money is pumped into education, which results in a disparity in quality. Again, the Constitution is found wanting, not through malice or ignorance, but through the inability to see two hundred years into the future.

The precedent for an originalist view of the Constitution is offered by religious thought. The Bible is accepted as Gospel (pardon the pun) and God's wishes and intents are *deduced* therefrom. Originalists treat the Constitution with the same reverence. It, like the Bible, is indisputable and the basis of all laws and guidelines. The problem is that, despite its age, the Bible does not often have to deal with current events, while the Constitution increasingly does. Just in the last thirty or so years, issues such as recruitment of terrorists, free speech vs. privacy, global warming, gun violence, immigration, rules for the internet, abortion, etc. are testing our Constitution. In many ways, it has come up short.

And to return briefly to President Trump's contribution to licensing bad behavior, which is usually laced with bullshit, think about the way he has "wink winked" to bigots in our country. Mexicans are rapists, black immigrants from Haiti and Kenya are from "shithole countries" (unlike those from Norway), black football players who protest violence against minorities are "sons of bitches." Anyone who is brown is bad, but the white supremacists who protested at Charlottesville were treated with false equivalence.

Yet his base, the 30-40% of the population that loves him unconditionally applaud this way of behaving. In response to the "shithole countries" speech, "supporters of the former businessman and reality TV star erupted in applause."[34] And, predictably, the other side has sunk to his level. Robert De Niro, the actor, said at an award presentation: "This f------ idiot is the president. It's The Emperor's New Clothes -- the guy is a f------ fool ... our baby-in-chief -- the 'J-------in-chief' I call him."[35] (Don't hold back, Robert.)

---

[34] Malone, Scott. "Trump's profanity delights supporters, horrifies etiquette experts." Reuters, 1/12/18.

[35] Daru, Deena, "Robert De Niro unleashes profanity-laced rant against Trump." CNN Politics, 1/10/18.

9: HOW TECHNOLOGY HAS ALLOWED BULLSHIT TO FLOURISH

Hearken back 100 or so years, to the earliest days of the twentieth century, when people actually knew the meaning of the word "hearken." No radio, no television, certainly no computers. The height of rapid communication was found in telephones, which were still not in everyone's home and expensive to use, especially over long distances. Most cars were owned by the wealthy.

Everyone's heard of the saying, "Don't shit where you eat." Back then, people shopped near their homes and interacted with people who lived close to them. Families clustered, either in small towns or in close-knit neighborhoods in larger cities. In these circumstances, a reputation for truth telling and honesty were necessary and therefore common. If you lied and were found out, you were known as "a liar." And then had to continue to interact with the people you lied to *as well as* the people who heard that you were a liar. Forever. *Propinquity discouraged dishonesty.*

Our reach has changed over the last hundred years. We can travel easily and interact with people at much greater distances. We are not "stuck," physically or virtually, talking to the same people over and over. While this is certainly a plus for a variety of reasons, it is also gives license to lies and deception. Our reputations don't follow us like they used to, and often unnoticed but serious consequences result.

I can lie to a woman I'm dating, saying that I'll call her when I have no intention of so doing. Or say that I'm really into her when I'm not, with the hope that I'll be able to "score." In the days of limited mobility, I'd have to face that young lady in class or in the neighborhood which would prevent that kind of lie for all but the most roguish of fellows. After all, she might have musclebound big brothers.

I can advertise that my widget is better than any other widget ever invented, whether that is true or not. In fact, it may be very difficult to sell *anything* without lying or exaggerating. In days of less mobility, if one owned a business in town, reputation was everything, so the urge to deceive was much lower. If you didn't provide a good service or reliable product at a fair price, or you cheated your customers, the word would get out quickly.

If I'm running for office, can I change someone's mind by truth telling? "Sorry, Mr. Doe, but your job is not likely to come back." "Your taxes, unfortunately, are likely to rise." I can say that if elected, I will fix the economy, whether or not that's true or even possible. To change the opinions of voters in my district, especially if I'm not the incumbent, I might be very tempted to deliberately or unknowingly lie, use tomfoolery, commit logical fallacies, etc. to get votes. If I am the salesman type, I might even be tempted to bullshit my way into office.

We don't even have to pretend to be *not* lying or bullshitting any more because few people will check and/or call you on it. If we lose the votes of the few people that do check, so be it. Most don't have the time, resources or knowledge to check on the truth of an assertion.[36]

We have come to expect bullshit and have become inured to it. In fact, some people even root for bullshit that comes from the mouth of a liar or bullshitter, as long as they have charisma or put on a good show. Not only is income disparity getting larger, but so is a factor that is highly correlated with it: educational disparity. As a guess, the less educated a person, the less able they are to resist the bullshit being flung at them.

We're not saying that everyone lies all the time, but more people lie or exaggerate or deceive more of the time with less chance of paying a consequence. It has just become very easy to get away with since we usually don't have to face the person(s) we've lied to and the sheer amount of information coming at us usually doesn't allow for fact checking. Reputations can be sculpted more than earned, and repaired if tarnished. That's why truth matters more than ever in

---

[36] Remember the "bullshit asymmetry principle."

the twenty-first century, and the need to be able to discern the truth is paramount.

It also doesn't matter whether the lying is intentional or not, or done consciously or not. We all follow our self-interest. If we lie and get a slap on the wrist in the form of embarrassment or censure, we are less likely to do it again. If we lie to get what we want and if helps us to get more of what we want, we are more likely to repeat the act.

10: THE MOST RELIABLE SOURCE OF PURE BULLSHIT

Professor Harry Frankfurt of Princeton argued that liars and truth tellers refer to the truth, but to bullshitters, the truth is irrelevant. "His eye is not on the facts at all…. He does not care whether the things he says describe reality correctly. He just picks them out, or makes them up, to suit his purpose."[37] Frankfurt's definition of bullshit implies that the speaker is not referencing or paying attention to the truth. But what if the speaker knows the truth, despite not paying attention to it?

Let's bring President Trump into the discussion. His expertise is in real estate and marketing/branding. If he is speaking on one of these subjects, he is sure to know what the truth is. Therefore, if someone bothers to fact check him, he will either find that Trump was telling the truth or he was lying. But what about other subjects?

Does the President know much about healthcare, tariffs, diplomacy, international affairs, or immigration, to name a few? The skinny is that he does not, and both his statements and behavior imply that he is ignorant of these issues. According to repute, he doesn't listen to advisers, at least those that don't

---

[37] ibid.

agree with him, and has infamously avoided the Presidential Daily Briefings in his early days in office. The result is that he came into office knowing little and through his intellectual isolation, has carefully maintained that meager level of knowledge. He doesn't read much, only listens to FOX News, and often parrots their opinions. He ostensibly[38] doesn't trust up-to-now reliable mainstream sources of information.

If a person doesn't know the facts, he or she cannot reference them, so that everything that comes out of their mouths, can be considered irrelevant to what is true. Trump comments repeatedly with the apparent intent of suiting whatever purpose obtains at the moment. He tells audiences what he thinks they want to hear, combined with things that make him look better. Thus, he only gives speeches in Trump-friendly states, usually promising that he will make their lives better by bringing jobs back and touting things that he has done for them. Because he is entertaining, and his audience is either selected or self-selects to be in support of him (few anti-Trump people will be attracted to his rallies, for fear of violence), he is reinforced.

---

[38] The word "ostensibly" is used, because it is suspected that he knows which mainstream media are truth tellers, but if his followers believe those media, he is, in effect, toast. So he denigrates the media by crying "fake news," to create an alternate reality which fits in with what he wants to sell to his base.

The scary thing is that because he makes it up as he goes along, especially when he goes "off script," almost everything that comes out of his mouth can be classified as bullshit. A number he quotes, or a statement he makes must fit the situation. Thus 3-5 million people voted illegally because Clinton beat him in the popular vote. The attendance at his inauguration was larger than that at Obama's because he didn't want to come in second. The response to the tragedy after the hurricane in Puerto Rico was "amazing," because he didn't want to be blamed for ignoring citizens of the United States. There were good people on both sides in Charlottesville because he didn't want to alienate his right wing base. And he made up numbers to "show" that the U.S. had a trade deficit with Canada, when in fact the opposite was true, because it fits his narrative that every other country takes the U.S. to the cleaners.

The situation comes first, and then the "facts" follow to fit whatever is needed to make his argument. The truth is irrelevant to President Trump. *In effect therefore, almost everything that comes out of his mouth is bullshit.*

But let's be fair to him. If he knows the truth when he's bullshitting, the bullshit is also lies. If he doesn't know the truth, it's merely bullshit. For President Trump, it's very hard to believe that he believes that 3-5 million people voted illegally, that his inauguration crowd was bigger than Obama's, etc. He's not that stupid. So, we can conclude that his bullshit is also a pack of lies. We wouldn't want to shortchange him.

There's also another dimension, however; amorality vs. immorality. If a person does or says something wrong, but doesn't understand that it's wrong, that's amoral behavior. If a person does or says something wrong, but the person knows better, it's immoral behavior. We'll leave it up to the reader to determine which is true of President Trump.

11: THE LOGIC AND ILL-LOGIC BEHIND BULLSHIT

Though it may sound counterintuitive, there is logic behind bullshit. The link is not direct, however. We'll need to define a few terms as we go along. First, it is believed that all people are logical or, to be more specific, use *deductive and inductive logical processes* most of the time.

Deductive logic (or deductive reasoning) is a "top-down" process; that is, we start from the general with some assumptions and combine them to *deduce* a conclusion from them. If the premises are true, the conclusion *must* be true. For example,

> All men are mortal,
> Socrates is a man,
> Therefore, Socrates is mortal.

The first two statements are true, so the third, the conclusion, must be true and is arrived at by a *deductive logical process*. But what about…

> All men are elephants,
> Socrates is a man,
> Therefore, Socrates is an elephant.

Here, one of the premises is untrue (actually crazy), so the conclusion is false. But... *the crazy conclusion is also reached by a legitimate deductive logical process.*

Inductive logical reasoning, on the other hand, is a "bottom up" process. That is, we go from a specific instance or instances and generalize or predict a general conclusion. If on election day, Candidate A has twice as many votes Candidate B after 10% of the votes have been counted, we can predict that candidate A will win, but not with great certainty. It is a prediction or a statement of probability. If the two-to-one ratio holds after 90% of the votes are counted, we can be much more certain that our prediction will be correct.

The reader may have noticed a contradiction. How can we say that people are logical creatures and still think we are easily duped by people with agendas? Shouldn't we be able to tell when we are being hosed, lied to or bullshitted? Unfortunately, we are constantly exposed to fallacious arguments and inaccurate information. Think of just about any commercial on television.

Further, even though I believe that we are motivated by self-interest all or almost all the time, much of it is misguided, as when I go way over the speed limit to get someplace on time, or when I "protect" myself from failure by not applying for a job or asking someone out for fear of rejection. In other words, sometimes what I think is in my "self-interest" doesn't work out that way; it is clearly unhelpful. And although misguided self-interest keeps me in business as a psychologist, it is clear that this is another contradiction. If I am guided by self-interest, doesn't driving too fast contradict my self-interest? Can these confusions be resolved in some way? I think so.

While the *processes* within us are logical, what is entered into those logical processes are not necessarily right or wrong. They are beliefs, which can be true by degrees, be totally true or totally false, or be simply matters of opinion. Viz:

> Gary thinks that all Democrats suck,
> Joe is a Democrat,
> Therefore Joe sucks.

This is a (deductive) logical process reaching a logical conclusion. The second premise is true since Joe is proud to tell anyone that he is a Democrat. But the first premise is not true or false; it is a *belief*. When that belief, which is certainly open to question by roughly half the country, is combined with a verifiably true assertion, the logically arrived-at conclusion is debatable. (Especially by Joe.) So where in tarnation did Gary get that questionable belief from?

And suppose I hear from my neighbor that they can't afford their medical insurance because the price of their policy "skyrocketed" under Obamacare. (Skyrocketed is in quotes because the policy could've gone from $200 a month to $1000 a month, or it could've gone from $200 to $250 a month which they still can't afford because my neighbor is out of work.) Most people wouldn't like the rise in premium, but wouldn't use the term "skyrocketing" to describe the second situation.

I go to work the next day and, in the break room, I mention my neighbor's plight to the guys. My coworker Fred says his sister-in-law's brother also got killed by Obamacare, and Tim says he knows someone in the same situation. When I hear some politician saying that Obamacare is a "disaster," it quickly and easily becomes part of my belief system.

Notice that this healthcare example produces a belief by an *inductive* logical process rather than a deductive one. I hear snippets of information which are anecdotal from three people and *induce* (or predict) that Obamacare is a disaster for everyone in the country. It doesn't matter that my neighbor's statement to me might be an exaggeration, or Fred's story might be a lie produced by repetitions of a story concocted by someone with a political agenda, and Tim might've just added his two cents so as not to feel left out of the conversation.

My belief is a probability statement based on the anecdotal stories of two (maybe three...you never can trust Tim) people that I know. And once that belief is formed and repeated to others, it is almost immutable, because I can't flip flop or I'll look like...a flip-flopper. Why do I take pains to avoid flip-flopping? I'm protecting myself from being ostracized for doing so. That's self-interest and has nothing to do with the truth or falsity of my belief.

Going forward, my newly formed belief can be used in a *deductive* logical process. Now, I can argue as follows:

> Obamacare is a disaster,
> Dave likes Obamacare,
> Therefore Dave is a disaster (really "Dave is just an idiot")

So are the contradictions resolved? Notice that the "All Democrats suck" premise didn't come from within the person; it was somehow gleaned from information available to me; perhaps from a book or magazine article; from listening to one-sided network news; from hearing Dad preach at the dinner table. In other words *that premise came from outside of me*. As did the three stories of people losing their healthcare that led me to induce "Obamacare is a disaster." So yes, the contradictions are resolved with the assumption (deduction? conclusion?) that what goes on inside of us are logical processes, but *the information we ingest to put into those logical processes are merely beliefs,* which can be opinions which are true, false, or anywhere in between.

And *although some conclusions that we reach are based on inaccurate information that seems illogical, the process actually involves deductive or inductive (or both) logical processes that are acting on inaccurate or totally false premises.* As they say, "Garbage in, garbage out."

How can we improve the accuracy of the information that is pushed at us by people or organizations with their own agendas? In other words, how can we filter out the bullshit? To do this, we need to be familiar with, and deeply understand, the logical fallacies, or ill-logic that others use to *influence* our beliefs. If other people are taken in by bad arguments, such as "Obamacare is a disaster," without solid evidence, that doesn't mean we have to suffer the same fate. We have to learn how to say, "Show me the proof," or "you can't say what you're saying from such a small sample size." We need retorts.

It is duly noted that only we can *control* which information we attend to, but others can and will try to *influence* us through shady or biased speech or behavior. Think of an athlete who fakes one way, and runs the other, trying to get the defensive player into making an error. There are a host of people trying to fake us out and get us to act in a way that's good for them but not so much for us.

The ignorance of we Americans is legion. Some examples, collected by a website called thoughtcatalog.com[39]:

Although a "relatively" high 40% of people were able to name all three of the United States branches of government — executive, legislative and judicial — a far lower percentage knew the length of a Senator's term. Just 25% responded that a Senator's term stretches for six years. Even less, 20%, knew how many Senators there were.

When asked in what year 9/11 took place, 30% of Americans were unable to answer the question correctly, even as few as five years after the attack. This was according to a Washington Post poll conducted in 2006.

25% of Americans were unable to identify the country from which America gained its independence. Although 19% stated that they were unsure, Gallup findings indicated that others stated answers

39 Lang, Nico. "14 Surprising Things Americans Don't Know, According To Poll Numbers." 10/7/13. thoughtcatalog.com.

varying from France to China. Older folks scored much better than young people on this question, as a third of those 18-29 were unable to come up with the correct answer.

Imagine the responses that would result if we conducted a "man on the street" interview and asked passersby to name three logical fallacies. I'd bet on blank stares. With rare exceptions, a course in logic is not taught in high schools. I took mine in college a hundred years ago and although I think I would know a logical fallacy if I tripped over one, their names don't exactly roll off the tip of my tongue. Part of the reason is that it is a hi-fallutin' off-putting subject, which quickly scares people away. The names of many of the fallacies are in Latin, which is Greek to most of us. And there is no easy way to catalog them; wikipedia lists formal fallacies (with subtypes propositional, quantification and syllogistic), informal fallacies (of which there are over 50 subtypes), faulty generalizations, red herring fallacies and conditional fallacies. Got that? (Neither do I.)

So I did some research on those pesky fallacies, with the idea of combining and simplifying them so that the average man on the street can wrap his or her head around them. The ultimate goal, of course, is to make us all better consumers, filterers if you will, of the information coming at us. If what we take in is more accurate, if we are less able to be duped by those with obvious or subtle agendas, then what we throw into the logical processes in our heads will be more accurate and the conclusions we draw will also be more on the money.

12: EARLY INTERVENTION

Please don't mistake the meaning of "early interven-tion," dear reader. A friend of mine[40] saw the title of this chapter and suggested that perhaps parents should sit their six year old down and say, "Timmy, the school called and told us that you bullshitted again! We have to nip this in the bud before you turn into a full-fledged bullshit artist by the time you're nine!" No, we're not that desperate yet. We are merely attempting to point out that, as obtains with every-thing else in life, the earlier you learn something the more it sticks with you and becomes a part of you. Recognizing and filtering bullshit is no exception.

Although this book is geared to adults, the best way to enable everyone to filter information for truth or falsity is to start early. I'm not alone in this belief. The following excerpt is from an article by Julia Belluz in Vox in early May, 2018. The article is a story about Dr. Mehmet Oz, who is a TV celebrity that has been accused of selling fake cures on his show, and who has now been appointed by President Trump to a council on children's health. (Yes, really.)

---

[40] Bob Cohen, who asked for attribution. If I were he, I would have made me promise *not* to mention his name.

"I have a modest proposal that might actually work to improve the health of the nation's children and help them avoid falling prey to the Dr. Ozes of the world: We should teach kids how to think critically about the information they receive from a very early age.

As I've written before, researchers from Europe and Africa recently worked to develop curricula — a cartoon-filled textbook, lessons plans — on critical thinking skills aimed at schoolchildren. In 2016, they tested the materials in a big trial involving 15,000 schoolchildren from Uganda's central region. The results of the trial, published in The Lancet, showed a remarkable rate of success: Kids who were taught basic concepts of how to think critically about health claims massively outperformed children in a control group.

This work is the closest thing we have to a recipe book for how to stop health bunk, like the stuff Oz peddles, from spreading. The takeaway from the research is clear: We must stop trying to change people's beliefs with facts, as all the Dr. Oz debunkers (myself included) have attempted to do. Rather, we need to teach people to spot bunk in the first place. If we did that, people like Oz, who mislead the public on health, would not hold the position they do in society. They would not be advising the president on important matters like children's health."[41]

Apparently the author has given up on us older folk and our attempt to convince other less enlightened adults that their beliefs are dead wrong. (Actually, the ones whose beliefs are wrong are the ones who I disagree with.) Instead, we should attempt to look to the next generation, and give them the tools to discern what is true from what is false and what are facts and what is "fake news." This makes perfect sense since the Left has gotten apoplexy trying to convince the Right, and vice versa, of the error of their ways for years. The only remaining audience worth addressing are the paltry few who are still in the middle.

---

[41] Belluz, Julia. "Dr. Oz is a quack. Now Trump's appointing him to be a health adviser." Vox, 5/4/18.

13: WORDS OF CAUTION

A few caveats are appropriate at this point. Although deductive and inductive logic operates within each of us, it does not prevent any of us from being ignorant, stupid or blind to the truth. Remember the "elephants" example? What about this one:

> President Trump is always truthful,
> President Trump says (*fill in the blank*),
> Therefore (*fill in the bank*) is true.

Not so fast. It should be evident that the truth or falsity of (*fill in the blank*) matters. As does the truth or falsity of the statement, "President Trump is always truthful." That's why the food fight between President Trump, who calls everyone else a liar, and the people that call *him* a liar is so important. We need to know real facts and not false facts. If the facts are, to be blunt, bullshit, they will *logically* enter into our thinking to produce conclusions that are bullshit.

So the topics of *logic, ill-logic and logical fallacies can't be viewed without consideration of the truth or falsity of our beliefs.* That is why, in 2018, at least in the political sphere, fact checking is so important. Is what we see on media news stations accurate or "fake news?" Is what we read in the New York Times or the Wall Street Journal biased or unbiased? Recognizing that bias exists by degrees, we need to be aware of the source of the news story and the way it is presented.

For those who want information about the leanings of any particular source of news, there is an amazing website called mediabiasfactcheck.com[42] that classifies major news sources into five major categories: left bias, left-center bias, least biased, right-center bias and right bias. This site also has categories for pro-science, conspiracy pseudo-science and questionable sources. Each category contains about 100 entries. As expected, both MSNBC and CNN have a left bias and FOX and Breitbart have a right bias. NPR, the New York Times and the Washington Post have a left-center bias. The Wall Street Journal, Washington Times, New York Post and Forbes have a right-center bias. Those that were rated "least biased" include the Economist, the Congressional Budget Office, Doctors Without Borders, Reuters and Pew Research.

The same site also conveniently lists the ten best fact checking websites.[43] All of them appear on the "least biased" lists. They recommend politifact.org, factcheck.org and OpenSecrets.org for political fact checking and snopes.com for checking urban legends. Those who want to be taken seriously in political dis-

---

[42] https://mediabiasfactcheck.com/2016/07/20/the-10-best-fact-checking-sites/

[43] ibid.

cussions and anyone, teacher or parent, who is in the position of instructing youngsters about civics and our political system needs to be familiar with these sites. And if anyone is dubious about the fairness of these websites, well… tough noogies.[44] If you are skeptical enough to believe that facts have a liberal bias, send this book back to Amazon.

A second caveat involves the question of how we can assert that people are logical creatures and, at the same time, write a book say that logical fallacies are all over the place. To make sense of this appearing contradiction, we have to bring in the concept of self-interest. Consider these:

> If I am a car salesman, it is my self-interest to sell my brand of car. And I will have a reason why the other brands, though maybe not terrible, don't quite measure up. Truth is irrelevant.

> If I am running for office as a member of the _____ party, I choose my stances, which mostly agree with the party line,

---

[44] A noogie, according to Merriam-Webster is "the act of rubbing one's knuckles on a person's head so as to produce a mildly painful sensation" as in "The boys gave each other noogies." But M-W states that the first known use was in 1968. I beg to differ. I was giving and getting noogies by the mid-1950s and I'm sure I wasn't the first since older boys in day camp taught me the technique in vivo.

and then I cannot and will not flip-flop on an issue. That's kryptonite to my candidacy. Whether I agree with what I say, or am lying through my teeth, doesn't really matter. My future career, reputation and income depend on me sticking to my guns.

If I buy something that I know strains the household budget, and I tell my spouse that it cost $30 when it cost double that, there is no way that I will, at some later point in time, fess up, unless my spouse confronts me with the receipt, which had been crumpled up and, not so craftily, placed in the recycling. If caught, I will say that is was an "honest mistake," apologize, and vow to never do it again.

If I am being paid to advertise a particular new drug, I will smile and say that the pill saved my life. If I am paid to sell certain insurance or mutual funds, there are none better, or if it is laundry detergent my clothes have never been cleaner. Again, truth is irrelevant.

If my neighbor is critical of, say, the quality of wood I selected for my deck, I will be very tempted to criticize his deck, perhaps saying, "Yours doesn't seem to be holding up too well." Now he may be totally right about the wood I selected, which I bought because of its low price, but I change the subject with my comment. I was being irrelevant, perhaps to save face and not have to admit that I'm pinching pennies.

All of these examples involve saying or doing something that *we think* is in our self-interest, regardless of whether it is true or false. Much of the time we stretch the truth to make money, at other times it's to protect us from embarrassment or shame or to win (or not lose) an argument. Sometimes we come to see what we are saying (or selling) as the truth; at other times we know we are prostituting ourselves to make a buck. And since self-interest is omnipresent[45] and is the crucial motivator for us logical humans, it is the reason logical fallacies are so commonly used.

---

[45] See Gribin, Anthony. Selfonomics: How Broadly Defined Self-Interest Explains Everything 2014, ttgPress. Also: Gribin, Anthony. I Am An Echo Chamber: The Basis Of Tribalism. 2018, ttgPress.

14: ARE ALL ADVERTISERS LIARS?

Groucho Marx once quipped, "I don't want to belong to any club that will accept me as a member." Though ironic and funny, it contains a lot of truth, especially as it applies to advertising. Would you want your opinion to be swayed by anyone who is trying hard to sway your opinion?

Why are products advertised? (This is *not* a hard question.) Someone wants you, yes you, to buy something. Are they looking out for *you* or for *themselves*? (Another softball.) By definition, the advertisers are looking out for themselves, usually to make money, sometimes to get you to give money to their cause, or sometimes to get you to believe a certain policy or politician. Is it good for you as well as them? Maybe, maybe not. It doesn't necessarily matter to them.

Logical fallacies are rife in advertising. Remember, they're trying to get you to buy a product that (a) you really need but you're not sure their brand is the best for you, or (b) that you don't yet know you need until they convince you that you can't live without it. Advertisers will do anything that is not illegal to get you to choose their stuff. (They only care that it's legal because they don't want to be sued.) Let's face it, telling the truth doesn't always pay. Imagine, "Use Zowie Detergent: it gets your clothes clean most of the time!" Or, "Get behind the wheel of a Fernmacher: the car that reliably comes in fourth in class in Consumer Reports!"

So they have to take facts and ignore them, or perhaps twist them until they are unrecognizable. A great example is the recent run of commercials for Alfa Romeo. One features pictures of their three models, all in fire engine red, with an overdub of a sultry female voice saying something like, "If you don't want to fall immediately into love, look away. ...If you don't want to be seduced, then please, please [she's really begging here], look away." A second ad in the series has an Alfa sedan and an SUV sliding gracefully around each other on ice to romantic music with an overdub, again performed by a sultry female voice, singing, with a great deal of tristesse, ..."I don't want to fall in love [long pause] with you.

In the interest of full disclosure, although I love Italian food, I don't particularly like Italian cars, since my 1968 Fiat blew its engine on the first day of ownership because the dealer forgot to put oil in (they replaced the car), its gas pedal fell into the floor, the steering wheel came off in my wife's hands and it wouldn't start in temperatures less than 32 degrees. I find the Alfas reasonably attractive nonetheless, but the ads really have nothing to do with their quality. And that's probably the point. Alfa cherry-picked its best quality, styling, and highlighted it, leaving out other parameters such as price, reliability, mileage, longevity, etc.. Can't say that I blame them, but the buyer has to be beware.[46]

An excellent article analyzes the fallacies in a host of commercials.[47] One example is provided by a good looking male model selling Old Spice after shave lotion. Some of the fallacies they list are ad hominem, non-sequitur, and false analogy. Without defining these (yet), the ad uses humor (your girl doesn't want you to smell like a girl) and attractiveness to convince men that they can get a woman by using their product. When I was young, I didn't find this task very easy, regardless of my choice of cologne. But then, I never did try Old Spice.

The message is…don't believe any advertisement! Well then, how do you buy anything at any time? By focusing on *your* needs and only your needs. Commercials for cars are all over the place and may make you aware of the various brands for sale. But you have to do your own due diligence. First narrow your search down by price range and, perhaps, beliefs that you hold. For example, if you believe in "buying American," you have to decide whether buying a Toyota which is built in the U.S. qualifies as within your category. If it doesn't, then your choice may be

---

[46] Personally, I'd buy the extended warranty, and make sure it covered steering wheels.

[47] Ward, Megan. Prezi @ https://prezi.com/wj7woufp9srz/logical-fallacies-within-advertisements/

limited to GM, Ford and Chrysler (then you have to find out if the model you want is built in the U.S. or, perhaps, Mexico or Canada, and shipped in).

Wait… you're not finished. You have to decide on a price range that's affordable to you. Here again, you are open to being hocus-pocused. If you buy a car, you want to compare "out the door" prices, which include not just the car, but the delivery charge, registration fees, tax on the vehicle and the cost of the salesman's wife's weekly visit to the nail salon. The price may look good for just the car but when these "extras" are added on, the total may be a lot more than you expected.

Leasing a car is even more difficult to get the straight poop on because it's really easy to obfuscate the cost to the buyer. For example, a Google search reports that one can lease a base model 2018 Honda Accord for $199/month 36 months ($36,000 miles) with $2,499 due at signing. First of all, the deposit works out to $69/month, so the price is now $268/month. If you want to upgrade to the next level, it's more. If you add any options, it's more. Then you pay sales tax. Another way to think about it is why would the dealer want to lease a car to you, if he/she didn't make *more* money than selling it to you? In a way, they get to sell the car twice; once to you, the first buyer, and then to a second buyer when your lease expires. They make money on both sales.[48]

The lesson here is that advertisers want to sell you something for which you may or not be in the market, that they are not looking to do you any favors, that they will play up the best feature(s) of their product (cherry pick), and that they will overlook or obfuscate the negatives (or outright lie) about them if possible.[49] So… should you pay attention to advertisements? It is recommended that the only use of an ad is to put a product on your radar screen. For example, if the Alfa Romeo commercial seduces you, fine, put it on your list. But pick three other cars to compare on a number of dimensions, such as price, attractiveness, economy, etc. and then do your research in Consumer Reports, the web and dealerships where you can test drive the cars. Whoever the guy was who invented the

---

[48] Edelman, Ric. @ https://www.edelmanfinancial.com/financial-planning/to-buy-cars-and-homes

[49] We have to concede that most advertisers will play within the rules, such as when drug companies recite the mandatory list of side effects of their miracle cure. They probably hope the list is long so that they can read them quickly and you won't listen; e.g., side effects of this product may include, but are not limited to… constipation, diarrhea, sleepiness (no fork lifts, please), sleeplessness, depression, anxiety, blah, blah, blah. Consult your physician or mortician if any of these occur. A related practice is the long disclosure that appears on websites or software, where you have to click "Agree" to continue to use the product. The only person that ever read this is the person who wrote it.

saying, "Let the buyer beware" was pretty smart.[50]   I bet he never bought a Fiat. As the reader may have surmised, I have P.F.T.D. (Post-Fiat Trauma Disorder).

---

[50] I wonder how many times he got taken before that saying came to him.

15: ATTACKING THE PERSON

Practice saying the word "irrelevant." You're going to use it a lot. Suppose you come home from work, starved, and desperate for dinner. You find your wife sitting on the couch, reading a book. You say, without any attitude, "What's for dinner, hon?" With her eyes still riveted on her book, she mutters, "Well, if you were less demanding, maybe I'd feel more like cooking." To which you say, "Irrelevant." No, you probably don't want to say this. You'd be sleeping on the couch for a week. But at least you should think it and understand why it's appropriate.

Why? Because your wife changed the subject and attacked you. It may be true that you are too demanding. But that's a discussion for another time. You simply asked about dinner. An appropriate response would've been, "Look, I had a tough day and I'm exhausted. Why don't we order Chinese?" This response stays on the topic.

Note that in a two person situation, attacking the person may be a reflexive and thus unplanned move. If the wife in the first example has had a terrible day, she's upset and might take it out on the first person who enters her view. When the husband asks about dinner, she may be thinking "I just sat down for the first time today, and now he wants me to make dinner." Reflexively she accuses him of being demanding instead of explaining her plight.

When you attack a person to change the subject, this is called "ad hominem,"[51] which is a very common logical fallacy. It can be anywhere from quite obvious to extremely subtle and involves discounting what another person has said because of a personal characteristic they possess, such as their gender, marital status, race, religion, political leaning etc. The general form of this fallacy is:

People who are _____ are wrong/bad,
John is a _____,
Thus, whatever John says is wrong/bad.

Whatever John says might be true or not true, but it should be evaluated on its merits, not the _____-iness of the speaker. If John says that on average, women are shorter than men or have longer hair (again on average), he is correct.

Some examples:

---

[51] This is reminiscent of Jackie Gleason, on "The Honeymooners" show from the 1950s. When his character, Ralph Kramden, was caught in a lie and couldn't think of a quick response, he would utter, "Homina, homina." An example is available at, https://www.youtube.com/watch?v=wK9ods-Wwflo

You try to give advice to a friend about marital (or child-rearing) issues and he responds by saying, "How can you give me advice on marriage (or child rearing) when you aren't married (or you don't have kids)?" He just changed the subject. You should know his comment is irrelevant. You may or may not know what you're talking about, but the advice you give should be evaluated on its merits and not summarily dismissed.

As with the dinner situation between the couple, this is a reflex reaction. We all tend to compartmentalize, by degrees, where we go for accurate information. We trust doctors with medical questions, accountants for tax issues, and other married friends (or parents) for advice on marriage (or child rearing). Nonetheless, an unmarried or childless person might have a different or interesting perspective about a subject because they can see it from a distance.

Politician Jane argues that Medicaid and welfare benefits need to be expanded. Her opponent points to her garish gold jewelry and discounts what she says because she is obviously wealthy and therefore can't understand the plight of the poor. The listener should recognize that Jane's wealth is not relevant to her argument. Both poor and wealthy people can empathize with the less fortunate.

Consider what must be in the mind of the critic. It is extremely likely that either the opponent is jealous of Jane, or realizes, especially in today's political climate, the intellectual and moneyed elite are resented by a large portion of the populace, so that using her wealth to attack is likely to be a winning strategy.

Phil believes that Republicans (or Democrats) are on the wrong side of every issue. He learns that his friend Barry is a registered Republican (or Democrat) and disagrees with him on everything. In Phil's mind, Barry is wrong because he is associated with Republicans (or Democrats).

This is inductive reasoning on Phil's part. If all Democrats are wrong on everything, and Barry is a Democrat, the Barry is wrong on everything. The problem is that if there were say a dozen issues, Phil might actually agree with Barry on several of them. On balance, Phil is right; that is, he will disagree with Barry most of the time. Note also that this has nothing to do with who is correct about any particular issue. Odds are they are both right on all issues, but for different reasons.

Any time, someone changes the subject and/or criticizes a characteristic of the speaker, rather than the issue under discussion, the word "irrelevant" becomes instantly useful. What the personal attack or subject-change does, in effect, is to present a *second* issue to consider. And two people can only discuss *one* subject at a time and get anywhere. If person A is talking about healthcare, and person B is talking about A's bad breath, how can they solve anything? Person B may be correct that A could use some mouthwash, but that is in no way related to healthcare. (Unless halitosis is considered a life-threatening illness.) They talk over each other. And, of course, if B attacks A in some way, you can be pretty sure that A will come back at him. Then where are we? In a food fight. To avoid this, A has to realize that he's being attacked by B, or that B is trying to distract from the subject or kidnap the conversation, and assertively exclaim, "Sir (or Madam), that's irrelevant!"

16: SOME PEOPLE ARE SAYING...

Suppose I don't like Jim. But I've been taught not to bad mouth him or anyone directly because it is rude and if I bad mouth Jim to Ralph, Ralph might figure out that I bad mouth him too when he's not around. Ah... but there's a perfect solution. I just say, "You know, I've heard people saying that Jim is a liar." Or, "Someone close to Ralph told me that he lies like crazy, so be careful when you deal with him." In these situations, I'm kind of doing Ralph a favor, cluing him in about Jim, but the information is not coming from me. I'm just being a good friend. By not being the source of the bad news, I can't be seen as the trash talker or the bad guy. And unless I'm willing to reveal my source, which is highly unlikely, especially since I made up the story, I can't be held accountable. Perfect solution, no?

Or how about if I say, "Hey Ken, I heard down at the club that your wife has been running around on you! I don't know anything myself, but if it's true you've got to do something. You're going to look like a fool..." If Ken asks me to reveal my source I take umbrage in not really knowing, having just overheard a conversation. Or I can say, "I'm sworn to secrecy. I only told you because I like you and don't want you to look like an idiot."

Unfortunately it's been used repeatedly by President Trump. Some examples: "An 'extremely credible source' has called my office and told me that Barack Obama's birth certificate is a fraud."[52] He even said he had sent investigators to Hawaii to determine the truth. Now we know for sure if they had found anything positive we would've been told, so we have to assume that either (a) they found nothing and he didn't want to admit it or (b) he flat out bullshitted and lied about the whole thing. (Remember, bullshit is false information made up on the spot to fit a narrative.) Given his subsequent record with truth telling, we'll go with (b).

Then there was the way he brought up and dwelt on the subject of Ted Cruz's citizenship. Cruz was targeted because he was Donald's closest rival in the polls and in the delegate count at one point in the primaries leading up to the 2016 Presidential election. "I'd hate to see something like that get in his way," Trump said. "But a lot of people are talking about it and I know that even some states are looking at it very strongly, the fact that he was born in Canada and he has had a double passport."[53] Trump never mentioned

[52] Marie-Claire magazine, May 4, 2016. http://www.marieclaire.co.uk/blogs/550112/donald-trump-quotes.html#yWAf1ip3D0y8Hr0H.99

[53] Taken from an article by: Epps, Garrett. "Ted Cruz Is a Natural-Born Citizen" The Atlantic, 1/14/16.

who the "people" were who were talking about it or the "states that are looking at it very strongly." In fact, the rumor, which Trump started, was debunked quickly and often by all media, but the seed had been planted.[54] Trump tweeted: "Ted Cruz was born in Canada and was a Canadian citizen until 15 months ago. Lawsuits have just been filed with more to follow. I told you so."[55] At some point he even said that Cruz was an "anchor baby."

"Some people are saying" is one of our President's favorite logical fallacies. "Indeed, this is exactly Trump's M.O. with literally every conspiracy theory, including the especially insane one that Ted Cruz's father was involved in JFK's assassination, is to say, 'Hey, I'm just bringing up concerns other people have.'"[56]

The lesson here is that if you hear anything bad about someone or something, where the source is anonymous, your first reaction should be to *not believe it*. Then question the motives of the person who is telling you. The formal name for this fallacy is "appeal to anonymous authority." It is a particularly insidious way to lie in order to deceive an individual or a whole

---

54 Remember Brandolini's Bullshit Asymmetry Principle.

55 From Twitter, 1/16/16.

56 Wolf, Leon H. "Called it: Trump Implies that Hillary Clinton Killed Vince Foster." Red State (newsletter), 5/23/16.

group of people. And often, it is used to destroy someone's character or career. It is almost always a prototype for bullshit.

17: KNOW IT ALL

In this fallacy, a person claims to know everything about a situation when total knowledge is clearly impossible. An example is if a husband says to his wife, "I know what you're thinking." No, he doesn't. He can't. He cannot be inside her head.

Religions make good use of this fallacy, in that a religious leader will speak for God, perhaps saying, "God wants us to love thy neighbor (or turn the other cheek)." There may be a good reason to get along with your neighbor or not get upset at small insults, but this is fallacious speech. A religious leader can't know what God wants. If anything, it's the other way around.

President Trump has been guilty of this one too. "Nobody knows the system better than me, which is why I alone can fix it," is a direct quote from the 2016 Republican National Convention in Cleveland.[57]

A related fallacy is when we assume something about everyone, as in "Everyone knows that the earth revolves around the sun." Sadly, one in five Americans believe that the sun revolves around the earth.[58]

---

[57] Marcus, Ruth. "Trump said, 'I alone can fix it.' How wrong he was." Washington Post, 1/20/18.

[58] Crabtree, Michael. "New Poll Gauges Americans' General Knowledge Levels." news.gallup,com, 7/6/1999.

Or, "Everyone knows that smoking leads to cancer." While 9 out of ten do, that's not everyone.[59]

Since no one can know everything about everything, we need to assess the qualifications of the person making the statement and the source of the information that is being conveyed. If a doctor advises me on a medical issue, I'm all ears, but if he is touting me on to a car that he loves, I need to take it with a grain of salt, since he probably is wealthier than I am and can afford a fancier car, only drives it 8000 miles a year and so can lease (while I drive 25000 miles a year and thus can't), may favor form over function, and may not care about fuel efficiency.

We also need to know, in certain situations, who provided input to the speaker. If President Trump only confers with his family members about certain issues, I may doubt the validity of his claims, or if I disrespect his advisors on economic issues, it is likely that I will not like his decisions on, for example, taxes, tariffs and international trade. President Trump is widely reputed to rarely take briefings from qualified experts and often "goes with his gut" with input from no one. If we remember the maxim, "garbage in, garbage out," if President Trump gets no input from reliable experts,

---

[59] Moore, David W. "Nine of Ten Americans View Smoking as Harmful." news.gallup.com, 10/7/1999.

then what comes out of his mouth is likely to be neither reliable nor expert.

18: RATIONALIZATION (EXCUSES)

When confronted with irrefutable proof that President Trump lies on a regular basis, some people will say, "Well, the Democrats are worse."[60] Sometimes, when an argument is shot down decisively, a person cannot or will not give in. This can happen either because that argument is central to who they are that giving in would turn their belief system into a collapsing house of cards, or perhaps because their ego won't allow them to be wrong or give in (or both).

So they "pull in" a peripheral construct or another argument which changes the subject and allows them to cling to their central belief. This argument is a rationalization, which is "the action of attempting to explain or justify behavior or an attitude with logical reasons, even if these are not appropriate."[61] In other words, they pull in a peripheral construct that *justifies* their original belief.

A clear example of this is common in the gun control debate. When faced with any clear evidence that guns, be it that there are too many of them, or that background checks aren't thorough enough or that automatic weapons are too easy to obtain, supporters

---

[60] French, David. "Mueller's Investigation Won't Shake Trump's Base." New York Times, Op-Ed, 10/30/17.

[61] Dictionary.com

will pull in parallel rationalizations such as "It's a mental health issue" or "We need a good guy with a gun to get a bad guy with a gun" or "Soon they'll be coming after all our guns." With these glib statements it becomes very easy to dismiss the concerns of gun control advocates, and resist any change in the laws.

Bigotry is also a topic which lends itself to rationalizations or making excuses. No one I know will admit to being prejudiced against minorities. If their actions belie their beliefs, they will say, "I'm not prejudiced, but…those people are lazy" or "they're criminals and rapists" or "they will take our jobs."

Income inequality provides a third example. Occasionally a wealthy person will be humble and admit that he's wealthy due to inheritance or even good fortune. But most rich people will rationalize their success by believing that the have-nots didn't work as hard, or made poor choices in life or that they don't have much talent or intelligence. If have-nots resent him, it is clearly sour grapes. These beliefs allow him to minimize any guilt that he feels for being comfortable as others suffer. Note that some of these beliefs may be true, but it is likely that inheritance and luck played a significant part in the overall picture and that once someone has accumulated wealth, the playing field is tilted in her favor.

All of these examples *seem* to represent ill-logic, yet the fact that calling in *correlated* beliefs to bolster one's argument maintains consistency in that person's belief system, which is a logical process. "I believe X. Joan said that X is wrong. But I also believe Y and Z, which are consistent with X and allow me to override Joan's "proof" that X is wrong."

19: EXPERT SHMEXPERT

LeBron James is a great basketball player. If he is talking about the game, I'm all ears. Recently, however, I've seen him in a Kia commercial. And although I have the utmost respect for LeBron's talents, I don't see him as an expert on cars, let alone Kias. The only thing that impresses me about that commercial is that he, at 6'9", can fit in the car. Actually that he can fit in any car.

But this attempt to refer to an expert of some sort has been around a long time before LeBron. Does anyone remember "Tony the Tiger" pushing Kellogg's Frosted Flakes? Tony, as is LeBron, is *irrelevant* to the quality or value of the product. If the reader remembers, you were warned to practice saying that word. "Irrelevant" is one of the most important words in the English language and the earlier we understand it and can use it properly, the better off we will be.

There are many versions of this fallacy. Sometimes the expert is an individual in power, or that has special knowledge, or is popular, or is a reference group of some kind. Some examples:

> Marriage has traditionally been between a
> man and a woman. Therefore gay mar-
> riage is wrong. No, traditional behavior

does not make something right (or wrong).

Jennifer Garner uses a certain credit card, so you should too. No, and even though you're gaga over Jennifer, she's being paid to get you to use that card.

Billions of people believe in God. Therefore God exists. No. That's not to say that God doesn't exist, it's just that the fact that so many people believe doesn't make it so.

Sally is a college professor and thinks she knows more than we do. Therefore, you can't believe anything a know-it-all like her says. No, she may be a know-it-all but what she says should be evaluated on its merit.

John gets worked up and emotionally defends his point of view, therefore it must be true. No, the emotion is irrelevant to the argument.

Candidate Sue says that people that attend her rallies are the smartest most knowledgable voters. Therefore they should vote for her. She's flattering her audience, hoping to get their vote. They support her at their own (vain) risk. Of course, since you also see yourself as extremely smart and knowledgeable, you can easily recognize Sue's feeble attempt to blow smoke up your you know what.

The popular kids in high school drink alcohol at parties. Therefore you should. No.

The lesson here is that an argument has to stand or fall on its own merits. Not on the reputation, power or agenda of the person presenting that argument. When someone is trying to convince us of something, we need to try and narrow our thoughts to the issue itself, and ignore the source of the message.

This fallacy has also been called "appeal to authority." It is up to the listener to determine whether the "authority" is legitimate or not. If a physician is giving a talk on diabetes, he is a legitimate authority so that what he says is likely to have validity. If, as in the above examples, Jennifer Garner is pushing a credit card or Tony the Tiger[62] is selling Corn Flakes, their recommendations are, at best, suspect.

---

[62] Tony must be at least 100 by now.

20: WIVES TALES

There are certain beliefs that are bandied about to convince people of a point of view or to sell something. Examples:

New Is Better. If you are trying to sell a product, using the word "new" in the sales pitch is intended to convey that it is better than the old stuff. This is not necessarily true. The company may have substituted cheaper ingredients in the newer version, they may have added an inert non-active ingredient so they could tout the novelty of their product. The new product might be more difficult to use, especially by older folks, if it involves technology. Or that because the old version was a family favorite, the new version gets a thumbs down.

That is not to say that the new product won't be better, it's just that it's not *necessarily* an improvement. You, the consumer, should have the final word.

Old Is Better. Another belief, which may be either true or false, is that old things are better than new. This usually involves choosing a way of behaving that is well-practiced and comfortable for the person. "I've always done it this way. Why should I change?" Or, "Life was better in the old days before the internet." These arguments are really matters of opinion and should be read that way. Old ways may be better for some people and worse for others. Yer picks yer poison.

Traditional is Better. This is often used to reject changes in social mores. Thus one may state that *traditional* marriage is between a man and a woman, thus rejecting gay marriage.

Natural Is Better Than Man-Made. In most cases, there is no evidence for this. Organic produce is all the rage these days. The evidence as to the benefits of organically grown food is still being debated.[63] It is clear that one downside is price; it is almost always more expensive than non-organic food.

Further, in some cases, belief in "natural" cures may prevent seeking more targeted and effective ones. St. John's Wort is recommended as a natural version of an antidepressant drug. Its efficacy is debatable, since its potency and targeting of depressive symptoms is variable and scattershot. If it keeps someone from going to a physician for a targeted cure for their emotional problems, it is a road block to a cure. The benefits and costs of natural and organic products should be evaluated carefully and not accepted at face value.

---

[63] Katz, David L. "Is Organic Food Better?" U.S. News Health, 9/4/2012.

21: CHARM THEIR PANTS OFF

This "fallacy" involves accepting someone's argument because they are charming, or charismatic, or just because you like him or her. Their charm, however, should be irrelevant to the weight of the argument they are trying to make.

Charming people are successful in many arenas. In politics, Ronald Reagan did some good things and some not so good things. So did J.F.K. What they both did very well is charm people. They were charismatic and people loved them. Bill "Slick Willy" Clinton was a smooth, likable convincing President, at least until the time when he got caught with his pants down, literally and figuratively. Al Gore lost the Presidency to George W. Bush largely because he was *not* charming, and W was the kind of guy you'd like to have a beer with. Hail-fellow-well-met.[64] Gore came off like a stiff snob.

Donald Trump won at least partly because he thrilled just enough more people than he turned off, and he ran against Hillary Clinton, who turned off just enough more voters than she thrilled. Call it charisma or showmanship, it worked for him. As listeners (or victims) of political arguments, we have to try and filter out the policies being espoused and the looks or

---

[64] Merriam-Webster: heartily friendly and informal .

charm of the person espousing them. This is often difficult since some people are just more likable than others.

Outgoing people tend to go into sales, or at least the ones who are successful at sales have to "put on the charm" or else they'll fail. Their job is to get us to buy their product, but we should know this and try to filter it out. Politicians and salesmen always have an agenda, which may or may not align with our own needs. If we know they're looking out for themselves, in one case to get elected and in the other to make money, we are forewarned and forearmed. Again, the word "irrelevant" fits.

There is no shortcut for doing our own research. Take the simple example of buying a car having only three alternative choice, say VW, Toyota and Subaru. If you listen to the upbeat, jovial car salesman at any one of these dealerships, they will try to convince you that their brand is the one you should choose. They have only one agenda: sell you *their* brand of car, whether they believe in it or not. They have to put food on their table. Their personality, or how likable they seem to be, as far as I know, will have little to do with how well your new car performs or how long it lasts.

Since all three of these brands are still in business, they each must have their benefits; i.e. there isn't one right answer, else we'd all be driving the same brand. The VW salesman may emphasize the engineering of the car, the Toyota lady might talk about reliability and the Subaru rep will talk about safety. And they might all be right. You, the prospective purchaser, need to do due diligence, weighing all the factors that are important to *you*, including price and style, and come up with a decision that is right for *you*.

If you don't do this kind of preparation, you'll be sold a car that resembles the Brooklyn Bridge by a salesperson who is likable and perhaps attractive. It would be a really good idea to ask yourself if your decision is being affected by these characteristics.

22: MY OWN ECHO CHAMBER

Confirmation bias occurs when people seek out information that is consistent with what they believe and ignore or avoid information with which they disagree. The result is that each of us creates and maintains an echo chamber, which consists of a network of beliefs within each of us that is quite resistant to change. Confirmation bias results in us believing that our religion, sports team, brand of car, and political preference is the right choice.

In the interest of full disclosure I, too, live in an echo chamber, which I find hard to escape. This is true for trivialities such as choice of restaurant and style of dress, to more important topics like politics and personal biases.

But I am a "truth seeker," aren't I? Why do I allow myself to not fight harder to escape my nexus of beliefs? One reason is that it is comfortable. That is, I generally like Italian restaurants and button down shirts and Democrats. Why should I strain to seek out other options? If it ain't broke, don't fix it.

Being comfortable with my beliefs allows me to see myself in certain ways. By way of example, I define myself as 1) a moderate Liberal, 2) anti-Trump, 3) pro-immigration and 4) for free trade. I'm comfortable with those descriptors. I'm guessing that anyone who knows me will see those four beliefs through what I say and do, and define me that way. That is part of my "personality."

Like most (probably all) people I have a desire to be, and be seen as, consistent. We need to see ourselves as having relatively constant beliefs and to have others see us that way. If our beliefs are changeable, the result is being seen as a pushover, wishy-washy, a flip-flopper, or a liar. Not that I want to change my opinions often, but if I do, the threat of external censure makes me think twice.

But there's one more factor that doesn't sit right with me. In the political sphere, at least, I take some kind of weird pleasure in taking in information that is anti-Trump and picking apart statements that come from pro-Trump sources, such as FOX News. It is very similar to, and may in fact be, schadenfreude, which is taking pleasure in another's misfortune.

The pleasure is similar to rooting for your favorite team and against their bitter rivals, but sort of in reverse, since I am primarily rooting *against* Trump (and his obviously misguided and/or evil supporters) and only secondarily *for* those who oppose him. It doesn't sit right with me because I can't recall detesting anyone in my whole life. Dislike, maybe. Detest, no.

So as far as my echo chamber of beliefs about Trump, I *don't want* to get out of it. I dutifully listen to FOX News on occasion, but look forward to what I call "trumptrocities" that appear on the nightly news at MSNBC or CNN. Nicholas Kristof, also addicted to Trump in a strange way, sees him as the light to which all moths are attracted, leaving little interest or energy in the media to focus on more important issues such as drug addiction and the suffering of people all over the world.[65]

The point is that a person's echo chamber, in its need to be consistent, searches for and inhales information that may be arrived at in a logically fallacious way. Some of us just want to be sold on information for or against a particular candidate or car, and don't care if it is accurate or not. The best we can do here is to be aware of what is in our own echo chamber, and if we are going to "drink the Kool-aid" once in a while, at least recognize it.

Another thing that is bothersome is knowing that someone on the other side of every issue is probably thinking the same way as I do. What if when Mitch McConnell sticks his finger in the eye of the Democrats, or when Paul Ryan enables Trump with his silence, or when Trump claims credit for something good that happened on his watch... what if the "other" not only feels good, but is happy that me and my kind are suffering!

---

[65] Kristof, Nicholas. "Our Addiction to Trump." New York Times Op-Ed, 5/5/18.

Unfortunately, the occurrence of schadenfreude among people I disagree with is not only possible, but likely. The nerve of those guys!

23: CHERRY PICKING

If you are trying to argue a point, it is tempting to pick one, or just a few, examples to show your opponent how right you are. No, no, no. Not fair. The other guy, we're sure, can find the same number of examples that support *his* view. This is "cherry picking," and the problem with it is that the number of examples is always small, and the choice of examples is anything but random.

To illustrate, suppose you flip a coin once and it come up heads. Can you conclude that the coin is "biased" in the sense that heads is a more likely outcome than tails? I hope you said, "No way." What if you flip it three times, and it comes up heads all three times? Or if you flip it ten times and heads comes up seven out of ten times? Again, the answer should be, "No, the coin is not necessarily biased." What we're really talking here is statistics. And within statistics, the concepts of *sample size* and *random sampling*.

The coin example is easily extended to situations in the real world. If you ask three people in the same area whether or not they think the Affordable Care Act is working, your answer will not be as reliable, in the sense of representing the attitudes of people in that area, as if you asked 100 people the same question. *The more people you ask, the more likely the result of your survey will accurately reflect the attitude of the whole popu-*

lation. The greater the number of people sampled, the higher the accuracy.

But there's another factor...randomness. If your "sample," meaning the number of people included in the survey, is chosen randomly, you are more likely to get an accurate reflection of the population. Suppose you ask 1000 people about whether they like or dislike the ACA, but all the people are from New York State. Or you did the same in Texas. If you want to make a conclusion about people from New York or Texas, this might work just fine. But if you want to come to a conclusion about the whole United States, the 1000 people must be selected randomly from all over the country. You might do this by throwing darts at a map of the U.S.A. 1000 times or, to avoid tendonitis, use a computer to choose your people.

In order to guard against falling for this fallacy, the listener has to take the opinions of individuals with a grain of salt. If John swears that his Hyundai is the best car on the road, you should listen, but realize that if he were correct, every car on the road would be a Hyundai and the other car companies would go out of business.

Presidents often try to sell this fallacy during their State of the Union speech. They'll invite half a dozen people who have benefitted from their amazing policies during their time in office and put them on display. It's very nice, especially for the proud parents of the ones who are showcased, but one can't draw any conclusions about the success or failure of the President's policies from this display. They might be great, but they also might stink. The sample size is way too small, and is anything but chosen randomly.

One of the most galling examples of cherry picking is a commercial promoting online gambling. The video portrays roughly three lucky players who won lots of money at this site (which will certainly not be named here), having started with very little. In fact the advertiser says that they'll give new players $20 for free! Imagine that! So there's a guy on the blurb, I'll call him "Happy Eddie," who proudly said, "I won $70,000 on _____ Casino." They left out the video of "Frowning Freddie," who might have said, "I lost $70,000 and my wife, my kids won't talk to me and does anyone have a couch I can sleep on?" This is cherry picking in extremis, and may lure innocent or gullible people into an addiction that can ruin their life. 'Nuff said.

24: CIRCULAR REASONING

If you make your case by starting with what you intend to conclude, it is a circular argument. Or if you restate the conclusion in another form, it is circular reasoning. You end up with what you start with or you start with what you end up with. Some examples:

You have to be crazy to see a psychologist, so anyone who sees a psychologist is crazy.

You have to have a screw loose to date him and you're dating him, so you must have a screw loose.

Gay marriage shouldn't be legalized because it's not socially acceptable. Why is it not acceptable? Because it should be illegal.

The Bible is the word of God. Therefore God is speaking to us through the Bible.

Republicans call Obamacare "a disaster." Why is it a disaster? Because Republicans have said it is from its inception.

The reader should be especially alert to this fallacy used in political arguments. For example, "…Because Mueller improperly stacked the deck of his special counsel staff with biased crusaders he transformed what was supposed to be an impartial investigation into an illegitimate and seemingly corrupt one."[66] The author starts out saying that Mueller's probe was biased and concludes that it was corrupt. Biased and corrupt have similar meanings so the argument is circular. (Note that the argument is valid, *if and only if* I grant the truth of the premise that the probe was biased.)

---

[66] Jarrett, Gregg. "Robert Mueller and his politically biased team of prosecutors need to go." Fox News, Politics, 12/9/17.

25: SAYING SOMETHING WITH WHICH NO ONE CAN DISAGREE

Political candidates want to say things that voters like. If voters dislike enough of what they say, the pol won't get very many votes. On occasion they will take a firm stand on issues, for or against this or that. But in between taking stands, it is best to say things with which no one can disagree. "We need to stand up for America," "We need to make our economy work for all people," and "We need to protect the rights granted to us by our Constitution" are examples. Marco Rubio, Republican Senator from Florida, in the speech that announced his candidacy for President in 2016, said:

> "If we create a 21st century of higher education that provides working Americans the chance to acquire the skills they need, that no longer graduates students with mountains of debt and degrees that do not lead to jobs…" Who can argue with those, Senator?

> "And that graduates more students from high school ready to work…" Ditto.

> "If we remember -- if we remember that the family, not the government, is the most im-

portant institution in our society…" Also tough to disagree with.

"By reversing the hollowing out of our military, by giving our men and women in uniform the resources, the care and the gratitude that they deserve." How can we disagree?

If a candidate is saying something that everyone agrees with, or that no one can possibly disagree with, the voter should ignore that statement. Try to separate the wheat from the chaff and figure out what they stand for and what they are against. The candidate is blowing smoke.

These statements are audience-pleasing and basically without importance or meaning. If a salesman says, "You deserve this (car/jewelry/cruise). You've worked hard all your life!" Of course you deserve it! Everyone on earth probably deserves that (car/jewelry/cruise). And most people work hard all their lives. So what? Deserving something is irrelevant. What's relevant is do you want it and can you afford it, and not much else.

26: CONSPIRACY THEORIES

When someone who possesses an immutable belief is confronted with contrary factual data, they have a need to pull in ideas that will allow this belief to continue to exist. The ideas that are pulled in are often, as an understatement, extremely weird.

Let's say Candidate X lost an election because he had policies that turned off too many voters. Avid defenders of X, who can't believe that X lost because of those policies, may devise scenarios about why he lost, usually with the implication that the election was stolen, perhaps because voting machines were tampered with or a foreign country intervened to help him lose. These stories, however improbable, are sometimes eaten up, repeated and spread by sympathizers of X. The notion that he was a rotten candidate or his policies didn't resonate with the voters don't occur to them. Though conspiracy theories usually fall apart on close examination, by the time they have been debunked, the information has been spread and the damage has been done. Just a few examples, plucked from wikipedia, include:

> "Pizzagate" was a theory that big shots in the Democratic party, including Hillary Clinton, were involved in child-sex trafficking, at a location called the "Comet

Ping Pong" pizza joint. Not coincidentally, this theory was spread by alt-right news sources, including Info Wars run by Alex Jones, in the run up to the 2016 Presidential election. Needless to say, it has been discredited countless times, but at the time, the damage had been done. Pizza joints may never be the same.

The "Deep State" is a theory that believes in the existence of unnamed elite "bad guys" who are running the country or controlling the government. Promoted by the usual cast of characters, Info Wars, Breitbart News and, as a result, President Trump, there has never been any substantiation from any source, though a Washington Post poll indicated that almost half of Americans believe in it. (Tinkers to Evans to Chance, today, would be Info Wars to FOX to Trump.)

There are people who believe that human contribution to the phenomenon of global warming has been made up to justify the continued employment of scientists or for some unspecified financial gain. Agreement among scientists that global warming is taking place is in the high nineties.

At other times, a conspiracy theory may simply evolve as a means to make money. "Qanon" is a conspiracy theory that began in November of 2017. Three techies got together and promoted this theory involving an unnamed high-ranking military member who supposedly leaked information about President Trump's secret "war" with Clinton supporters and Hollywood stars. Obviously, there is no evidence for this for any of this, but Qanon signs and supporters seem to show up at Trump rallies, without any discouragement from the President. "...the theory has been increasingly linked to real-world violence. In recent months, Qanon followers have allegedly been involved in a foiled presidential assassination plot, a devastating California wildfire, and an armed standoff with local law enforcement officers in Arizona."[67]

Sadly, it should be noted that Donald Trump seems to believe in all of the above con-

---

[67] Zadrozny, Brandy & Collins, Ben. "How three conspiracy theorists took 'Q' and sparked Qanon. NBC News, 8/14/18. https://www.nbcnews.com/tech/tech-news/how-three-conspiracy-theorists-took-q-sparked-qanon-n900531.

spiracies, as well as others that suit his needs. This puts him in an odd position; if he really believes in those conspiracies then he is just ignorant; if he is just supporting them to cater to his base he is a bullshit artist. If he doesn't believe in the conspiracies then he's just lying. Actually, he is all three.

President Trump is nothing if not inventive. Not only does he echo conspiracy theories, first offered by alt-right news sources such as Breitbart and InfoWars, he starts them himself and often does so *preemptively*. Readers will remember that before the election, he said that the voting was going to be rigged in the Democrats favor, that they would steal the election. "'Phony' polling and the colluding media 'refusing' to report on his imminent victory. Paul Ryan's backstabbing 'months-long campaign' to get Hillary Clinton elected president. Donald Trump and his supporters keep adding to their list of the dubious ways they've been boxed out from winning the White House."[68] "'You have 1.8 million people who are dead, who are registered to vote, and some of them absolutely vote. Now, tell me how they do that,' Trump told Sean

---

[68] Samuelsohn, Darren. "A guide to Donald Trump's 'rigged' election: Zombie Democrats, colluding reporters and backstabbing Republicans. Politico, 10/25/16.

Hannity on Fox News."[69] He also said that 2.5 million people were registered in two states and voted twice.

The purpose of the preemption is to both gin up his base so that they will go out and vote, simultaneously casting aspersions on his opponent, as well as to give him an excuse to challenge the result if he loses, in the process salving his ego. And of course, knowing that Trump is a conspiracy-enthusiast, FOX news, Breitbart, InfoWars and the National Enquirer have been eager to provide fodder for their most notorious and faithful client.

Needless to say, a person confronted with conspiratorial explanations for events has to approach the topic with a great deal of doubt and demand the factual basis of the claim. Conspiracy theories are used by people *out of the mainstream* who cannot make their point by resorting to facts. My belief is that many of them are really Martians, sent here to earth to destroy civilization. Go ahead; prove me wrong! And be careful where you get your pizza!

---

[69] ibid.

27: SCARE TACTICS

One particular form of conspiracy theory involves scaring the listener into being terribly afraid of something. The something will depend on the "achilles heel" of the listener. If I have children, telling me that if I vaccinate my kids against the usual childhood illnesses, they will develop autism, might scare the hell out of me. A bogus report by a doctor in the late 1990s made that claim with the result that many American parents didn't vaccinate, which endangered not only those children, but children that were exposed to the non-vaccinated ones. To add insult to injury, clinics in third world countries (Pakistan and Nigeria) were bombed when it was rumored that vaccination somehow threatened Islam.

Politics provides another playing field for scare tactics. If workers are worried about their continued employment, a politician can play this up by arguing that this or that group, usually foreign born and/or minority, will take their jobs. If other countries are taking advantage of our workers and industries, then "putting America first" is a welcome slogan to those whose livelihoods are threatened. Or the pol can promise to bring back jobs or claim to have kept a company from moving abroad by dint of his influence.

If I am afraid of violence creeping into the suburbs where I live, I am all ears when it comes to news about the plethora of guns in urban areas, or the ubiquity of MS-13, or Mexicans, who will rape and pillage if they get into our country. "President Donald Trump on Thursday referred to what was perhaps his most notorious comment during his 2016 campaign: calling Mexicans "rapists." Trump suggested that women traveling through Central America en route to the United States were "raped at levels that nobody's ever seen before. The comments come amid a flurry of media attention about a caravan of migrants traveling through Mexico. There is no evidence to suggest that any of the travelers have reported being raped on their journey."[70]

Note that the commonality among the examples above is that invoking fear in someone who is insecure in some way, softens the person up to believe in, and *actually want to* believe in, bullshit.

There are less odious, or at least more socially acceptable, uses of scare tactics. They are often used to promote healthy ways of living. Anti-smoking and anti-drug campaigns famously describe the catastrophic results of not quitting the habits. And of course there are a minority of religious leaders who use scare tactics to keep the flock close, as in, "If you

---

[70] Mark, Michelle. "Trump just referred to one of his most infamous campaign comments: calling Mexicans 'rapists'." Business Insider, 4/5/18.

don't believe in God, you will go to hell!"

The best defense against scare tactics is to determine the probability of the threat actually coming to fruition. Many studies have been conducted that find absolutely no link between vaccinations and autism. The promise of jobs is certainly welcome among those that are in fear of losing theirs, but do those promises actually come true, given a suitable amount of time, or was the promiser just bullshitting. And, as many studies have shown, Mexican immigrants commit crimes at a lower rate than American citizens, even according to the right-wing think tank CATO institute.[71]

Note that using scare tactics to promote health always has research and data to back up the claims being set forth. As to whether the threat of hell for nonbelievers is real or not, we'll just have to wait and see.

---

[71] Nowrasteh, Alex. "Immigration and Crime – What the Research Says." CATO Institute, 7/14/15. @https://www.cato.org/blog/immigration-crime-what-research-says

28: CLAIMING "FAKE NEWS" IS BULL-SHIT

Closely related to conspiracy theories is the concept of "fake news." The term seemed to originate to describe the output of a group of web-savvy young adults in eastern Europe, who posted totally fabricated stories on social media, especially on Facebook in 2016.[72] Examples are, "FBI agent suspected in Hillary Email leaks found dead in apparent murder-suicide" and "Pope Francis Shocks World, Endorses Donald Trump for President, Releases Statement."[73] The motivation for these placements appeared to be simply to make money from clicks on their postings. Since the American election was in high gear at that time, the stories that concerned that election attracted the most clicks, thus being their most lucrative efforts. But that was just the beginning...

In December of 2016, Hillary Clinton used the term "fake news" to refer to the "Pizzagate" conspiracy theory, a rather bizarre story which involved sex slaves, a pizza parlor named "Comet Ping Pong" and, of course, Democrats. But the most famous use of the phrase came into play when "President-elect Trump

---

[72] Oehlheiser, Amy. "This is how Facebook's fake-news writers make money." Washington Post, 11/18/16.

[73] ibid.

took up the phrase the following month, in January 2017, a little over a week before taking office. In response to a question, he said 'you're fake news' to CNN reporter Jim Acosta. Around the same time he started repeating the phrase on Twitter."[74]

Since that time, it has become one of President Trump's favorite plaints; he applies it to any news story that is critical of him or that he disagrees with, and especially those media reports that have to do with Robert Mueller and/or the Russia investigation. Left-leaning sources have taken it up as well, often using it to describe much information put out by the White House.

As he is wont to do with conspiracy theories, President Trump uses "fake news" preemptively, to inoculate his base against any reports that show him in a bad light. It also seems intended to discredit anything that comes out of Mueller's investigation, in case any of it is negative. Trump is very good at intimidating Republicans into not calling him out on his frequent egregious words and actions. By calling Mueller's efforts fake news in advance, he is likely hoping to soften the blow and keep a lid on objections from within his own party.

_____

[74] Wending, Mike. "The (almost) complete history of 'fake news.'" BBC News, 1/22/18.

"The desire to think the best of Mr. Trump combined with the deep distaste for Democrats grants extraordinary power to two phrases: 'fake news' and 'the other side is worse.' 'Fake news' erects a shield of disbelief against the worst allegations and allows a person to believe that Mr. Trump is better than he is. For too many Republicans, every single troubling element of the Russia investigation - including multiple administration falsehoods about contacts with Russian officials - represents 'fake news.'"[75]

Before we go one step further, let's be clear. *Claiming "fake news" is pure bullshit*, being disproved by two major concepts central to human nature: competition and self-interest.

To begin, think of competition in major league baseball. Baseball players move up through the ranks. From high school to college to the minors and, if they're good enough, the major leagues. It's a pyramid, and a steep one at that. The best of these are able to stay in the majors and the better they are, the more money they make and the longer their careers.

---

[75] French, David. "Mueller's Investigation Won't Shake Trump's Base." New York Times, Op-Ed, 10/30/17.

The same is true in other fields. The best high school students go to the best colleges. Kids who go to the best colleges, and do reasonably well, have the best shot at the best medical schools, law schools and STEM schools. If you make it through Johns Hopkins in med, Harvard in law and M.I.T. in tech, you've got a great career ahead of you, in terms of both status and income.

For journalism, some of the best colleges are Emerson (MA), U. Of Texas at Austin (TX), Northwestern (IL), U.S.C. (CA) and N.Y.U. (NY).[76] Students who graduate from these schools compete to get the most coveted jobs in journalism, which just happen to include the major newspapers in the country, among which are the New York Times, the Washington Post, the Los Angeles Times, the Chicago Tribune and a relatively small number of elite periodicals.

In journalism, as obtains with most other fields, competition assures that the well-known papers, listed above, hire the best and brightest and get almost every story quickly and accurately. If they don't, they will be "scooped" by another esteemed paper and their reputation will suffer.

Which brings in the second concept, that of self-interest. The editors of the mainstream media have

---

[76] https://www.collegefactual.com/majors/communication-journalism-media/journalism/rankings/top-ranked/

also reached the pinnacle through competition. They demand truth and accuracy from their reporters. Sources are checked and supported by collateral channels of information before they go to press. Occasional mistakes are retracted. They may have a liberal slant on things, but they *do not* make things up. The editors and reporters have too much to lose to play fast and loose with the truth. *The reward for spreading fake news is non-existent since others will unmask the act, and the cost of being a distributor of fake news is enormous. It's not worth the risk of losing a reputation, job or career. It is not in the self-interest of newspapers, editors or reporters.*

A recent example is provided by the "Strange Case of Nikki Haley's Curtains." On September 13, the New York Times first featured the headline, "Nikki Haley's View of New York Is Priceless. Her Curtains? $52,701."[77] This lead strongly carried the implication that Haley was responsible for the purchase of those curtains. Turns out she wasn't. On the 14th, the headline was amended to "State Department Spent $52,701 on Curtains for Residence of U.N. Envoy." And the following editor's note was at the top of the article:

An earlier version of this article and headline created an unfair impression about

77 Wemple, Erik. "New York Times wrongs Nikki Haley with curtain headline." Washington Post Op-Ed, 9/14/18

who was responsible for the purchase in question. While Nikki R. Haley is the current ambassador to the United Nations, the decision on leasing the ambassador's residence and purchasing the curtains was made during the Obama administration, according to current and former officials. The article should not have focused on Ms. Haley, nor should a picture of her have been used. The article and headline have now been edited to reflect those concerns, and the picture has been removed.[78]

The reader should take note of two things. First, that the Times retracted what the story implied about Haley, in effect offering an apology. And second, that the Post, it seemed, was only too eager to point out the faux pas, as were other news sources.[79] Competition motivated the Post's actions, and embarrassment was behind the retraction by the Times.

Contrast this with sources of (real) "fake news." While the legitimate sources have worked hard to get to the top, fake sources will be lightweights; relative

[78] ibid.

[79] Hannity, Sean (staff). "BUSTED! NY Times Suggests Nikki Haley Bought $52k Curtains, Actually Purchased by Obama Admin." At: https://www.hannity.com/media-room/busted-ny-times-suggests-nikki-haley-bought-52k-curtains-actually-purchased-by-obama-admin/

newcomers with all to gain from getting a story published and spread, and nothing to lose. In some cases the information comes from a kid with a computer trying to make spending money. Often social media act as "amplification," which "includes coordinated campaigns of likes, shares and comments from fake accounts, such as those set up by Russian-controlled organizations. These campaigns were conducted both on Russian-created posts and legitimate posts by news outlets and public figures."[80] The story is then picked up by InfoWars or Breitbart and magnified. FOX acts as a catalyst, having the power to reach millions of people. And then, of course, President Trump, who appears to be in a parasitic relationship with FOX, broadcasts the story to his millions of followers, who eat it up.

So how does a poor innocent news junkie see through the fog? The first step is to realize that *if a story seems weird and unlikely*, it probably is. If the story is not corroborated by a mainstream source, it is probably not to be believed. Since the claim of "fake news" is a defense maneuver without reasons as to why the news is fake, it should be disbelieved automatically. The odds are overwhelming that if someone claims "fake news!," they are lying through their teeth and

---

[80] Shapiro, Leslie. "Anatomy of a Russian Facebook ad." Washington Post, Business Analysis, 11/1/17.

bullshitting at the same time. Remember that bullshit is defined when the speaker does not reference the truth and makes something up to fit a particular situation. Thus *claiming "fake news" is an all-purpose form of bullshit. It can be applied to anything one doesn't agree with or opposes.*

So before you start spreading the juicy tidbit to all of your contacts, either by word or Facebook, do some checking. The way to check is to watch or read the legitimate news sources that are available to you including, but not limited to, FOX. Even if another major media outlet, such as the Times, Post, CNN or ABC is late to the game, they will check the story and broadcast it *if, and only if,* it holds water. By contrast, if you don't hear some version of the story from legitimate sources, it is bullshit, pure and simple. *Real news outlets will not let a truthful story go unreported.* Don't forget that most of this fake news is very similar to the headlines we used to laugh at in the National Enquirer such as, "Elvis Lives!" Or "Actress Bears the Child of an Alien!"

29: CONFLUENTIAL REASONS

It is often tempting to assume that the reason for an occurrence is simple; i.e. that there is *one* reason things turned out the way they did. Usually nothing is simple. An obvious example is in the dissection of the 2016 Presidential election with pundits positing why Hillary Clinton lost despite being a heavy favorite. Among the reasons offered were that she didn't campaign in crucial states (WI, PA, MI) enough due to complacency, that the Russians influenced the election, that James Comey's decision to reopen the investigation into her emails a week before the election tipped the scale, that she was a weak candidate, that she shot herself in the foot by using the word "deplorables" to describe Trump supporters, that the Clintons somehow profited from their charitable organization, the Clinton Global Initiative, etc.

While a few voters may have focused on just one of the above possibilities or another, most made their decisions based on a multitude of factors (put into a conscious or not conscious cost-reward matrix) which narrowed down to one possible action: vote for Clinton or vote for Trump (or one of the third party candidates).

We are not simple creatures. Think about the decision to purchase a car. Although a few of us will fall in love with the looks of a particular vehicle, and others will buy the cheapest one they can get, most of us weigh a whole host of factors before coming to our final decision. We perform some kind of cost-reward analysis in our heads, which will probably include price, styling, mileage, comfort, performance, safety, status, practicality, again among others, before making a final choice.

In History class we learn about the causes, plural, of the Civil War. historynet.com[81] lists thirteen, including the Missouri Compromise, the Abolitionist Movement, Slavery, Secessionism and Lincoln's election. All were contributory reasons, necessary but not necessarily sufficient.

If we are being honest with ourselves, think about the *whys* of our own behavior. There are very few actions that we take for which there is only *one* cause; running away from a fire comes to mind. If someone tells you that there is only one reason they voted for someone, or chose to live somewhere or take a particular job, you should be doubtful. They either aren't in touch with their own motivations or don't want to tell you what moved them. Self-interest is often a motivation that people hide, since it's not socially acceptable.

They might say they chose a restaurant because they thought you would like it, when in reality they

---

[81] http://www.historynet.com/causes-of-the-civil-war

wanted to go there, or it was close to their home, or it was cheap, or didn't have a liquor license. They might say they voted for Candidate A for policy reasons but may have incorporated the looks of the candidate (Sarah Palin and Mitt Romney come to mind) or the entertainment value of the candidate or even prejudice against a race or gender. In fact, given the growth of tribalism in our twenty-first century world, it would be surprising if racial prejudice and gender identity was not a contributor (by degrees) to most votes cast. The voter may not even be aware that these types of factors are part of their decision process, or if they are aware, may be ashamed and keep their own counsel.

The lesson is to listen when people give a single reason for their action, and try to figure out what other motivations (pluses) or roadblocks (minuses) entered their thinking.

30: CORRELATION DOES NOT MEAN CAUSATION

If two events are said to be "correlated," it means they seem to occur together. Can you say that one *caused* the other? Absolutely not. Event A might have caused event B, event B could've caused A, both events may have been caused by a third factor (C), A and B could cause each other (in circular fashion), A could cause another event (C) which then causes B, or the correlation could be a coincidence.[82] An example from wikipedia[83] is that if it is observed that people who go to bed with their shoes on tend to get up with a headache, it doesn't mean that one caused the other. It is likely that a third factor, going to bed drunk, caused both.

Looking at larger issues, if unemployment went down during Obama's tenure in the White House, it doesn't mean he can take credit for it or, for that matter, has any right to claim responsibility for it. He may have, but you can't conclude that. Similarly, if income disparity grew during Obama's terms, it doesn't mean that Obama caused it. He may have, but you can't conclude that either. One has to look at the specific policies implemented or supported during his Presi-

---

[82] See wikipedia listing for "correlation does not imply causation."

[83] ibid

dency (such as bailing out GM or pushing through the ACA) and then evaluate whether those actions had a positive or negative effect on the economy. There are many mitigating and extenuating circumstances, as well as the confluentiality of factors, that stand between correlation and causation. *When a politician blames another for causing vast negative changes in our society, watch out. They're almost surely committing this type of logical error* (called "cum hoc ergo propter hoc," Latin for "with this, therefore because of this.").

President Trump has provided us with many examples of this fallacious argument, seeming to claim credit for anything positive that has happened on his watch. Some examples that appeared in CNN Politics:[84]

> He restored the phrase "Merry Christmas." "The lengthy and brutal (and wholly imagined) 'war on Christmas' was over, he seemed to say, and -- thanks to him! -- 'our cherished and beautiful phrase' had finally scored a decisive win."

> He took credit for firing his business advisory boards when they actually quit be-

[84] Krieg, Gregory. "10 of the most questionable things Trump's claimed credit for." CNN Politics, 1/2/18. https://www.cnn.com/2018/01/02/politics/donald-trump-took-credit-for-what/index.html

fore he had a chance to do so. "When his business advisory boards began to unilaterally dissolve themselves in mid-August, Trump stepped up to see them out the door -- and tweet that their departure was his own doing."

He is responsible for the popularity of Lady Gaga. '"I really believe I had at least something to do with it,"' Trump wrote. '"She became a big star and maybe she became a star because I put her on the Miss Universe pageant. It's very possible, who knows what would have happened without it, because she caused a sensation."'

He is the one who started airplane rallies. '"Do people notice Hillary is copying my airplane rallies,"' he asked in a September tweet. '"...(S)he puts the plane behind her like I have been doing from the beginning."' Bush, Kerry, McCain and Romney did it before him.

Trump said he got rid of the birther issue. "When Obama released his long-form birth certificate in April 2011, Trump tout-

ed his role in "getting rid of this issue."'
'"We have to look at (the birth certificate),
we have to see is it real, is it proper,
what's on it, but I hope it checks out beau-
tifully,"' he said. "But the lie, and its
crude appeal to a certain segment of the
voting public, proved too dear to really let
go. Trump would peddle it for another
five years, before eventually backing off
and blaming the whole thing on Hillary
Clinton."

Trump took credit for airline safety during his first year of office. "The skies were
friendly to civilian travelers on commercial jets in 2017. Not a single passenger
flight crashed all year, anywhere. So in his
first volley of post-vacation tweets, Trump
on Tuesday applauded ... himself."

Thinking that one is the center of the universe is
a characteristic of the narcissistic personality, for
which Trump is the poster child. As will other narcis-
sists (such as Kim Jung Un), they claim credit for anything that goes well, and deny responsibility for anything that turns sour, blaming it on a real or imagined
foe. In Trump's case, he has a number of favorite
punching bags, depending on the day. Hillary Clin-

ton, Barack Obama, the news media, the intelligence services, the Justice Department, Nancy Pelosi, Jeff Sessions, the Dems, and anyone else that doesn't agree with him take turns being targets of his venom.

No one is omnipotent, so that if someone claims to be, the listener should question the motivation behind the claim and every word that comes out of his or her mouth. And please remember, if two things happen to occur at the same time, you can't claim that one caused the other.

31: HYPERBOLE (EXAGGERATION)

Hyperbole, n. [pronounced hyper-bow-lee] [from Amer. hyper- (overactive), and bull (bullshit), and lie (untruth).] An exaggerated, elaborated or embellished version of the truth. Usually harmless unless someone really believes it.
  -Webster's Unabridged Dictionary (not)

Here's a quiz, dear reader. Which great, tremendous and unbelievable famous person frequently uses the following words and phrases: great/greatest, tremendous, thousands of, bad, mess, disaster, terrible, unbelievable, winning? If you said anyone in the world except Donald Trump, you'd be wrong.[85] As exaggeration, hyperbole can portray things as the absolute best, or the absolute worst. What follows are two examples of the conversion of people that Trump doesn't like or agree with, into being the absolute worst.

Suppose you're playing basketball and your team loses. The guy you were guarding comes up to

---

[85] Cooper, Marta. "Donald Trump's great, tremendous, unbelievable penchant for hyperbole at the first presidential debate." Quartz, 9/27/16. @https://qz.com/792825/presidential-debate-donald-trumps-great-tremendous-unbelievable-penchant-for-hyperbole/

you and calls you "a loser," with no sign of a smile on his face. What would you do, or at least want to do, to this guy? Perhaps kick him in the basketballs? Well, Donald has done this more than a few times. In the political world losers, according to Donald, include Barack Obama, Chuck Hagel, Jeb Bush, John McCain, David Cameron and Karl Rove. In the media, losers include Arianna Huffington, Bill Maher, Bill Moyers, George Will, Brian Williams, Charles Krauthammer, Chuck Todd and John Heilemann. Celebrity losers include Cher, Stevie Wonder, Jon Stewart, Jay Leno, Rihanna and Rosie O'Donnell.[86] Gotta say he's fair though… no party or network or medium is left out. It seems that the criterion for being called a loser by Donald amounts simply to disagreeing with or standing up to him.[87]

Or suppose your boss says that not only are you incompetent, but you are the "worst" employee ever! That'll make you feel good, won't it? "Worsts" according to Donald include many of his former rivals for the nomination, including Ted Cruz, Marco Rubio, John Kasich and George Pataki, many minor Democrats such as Barack Obama, Bill and Hillary

[86] Gilmore, Scott. "The definitive list of every person Donald Trump has called a loser." MacLean's, 7/21/15.

[87] Taken from: Gribin, Anthony. Trump's Tricks: The Artful Use of Intimidation and Lies. ttgPress, 2016.

Clinton (separately), Bill De Blasio, and other public figures such as Mitt Romney and Anderson Cooper. We guess that Donald has very high standards. Here's a tweet that is a doozy: "Obama is, without question, the WORST EVER president. I predict he will now do something really bad and totally stupid to show manhood!"[88][89]

The astute reader might notice that the quiz and the quotes above are referenced from 2016. Needless to say, his use of hyperbole hasn't diminished since.

The odd thing about hyperbole is that it is that most of the time it is easy to pick up. Except when the listener wants the exaggeration to be true. Suppose you're a rabid Boston Red Sox fan. You watch or listen to as many of their games as you can, and live or die by their wins and losses. They make the playoffs. You're psyched. You go to your local pub to watch the game with like-minded fans. You are cheering for your team; your guys. They are the greatest and your feelings are echoed by the others in the bar cheering every hit and run. The Sox win and you leave the bar on a high.

---

[88] Tweeted by Donald on 6/5/14.

[89] Gribin, op. cit.

How much different is that scenario from the mood at a Trump speech or rally. Trump only holds rallies in friendly venues, like the bar in the Red Sox example. People who attend self-select, in the sense that if they are not pro-Trump they won't attend. Again, just like the pro-Red Sox watering hole. Trump gives his speech and revs up the crowd by saying things that he knows they want to hear. His sentiments are echoed by almost everyone in the arena. Unlike the baseball game, however, the end result is assured, since unlike the Red Sox, he can't lose. Attendees leave the arena on a high.

Just like Red Sox fans, or the soccer fans of any country in the World Cup, Trump followers are fans. Fans don't reason; they believe and they root. They will not shift their allegiance. Because they are fans, they not only don't see or mind hyperbolic speech, they crave it. And Trump being at heart a great entertainer, just like a great baseball team, is just what the doctor ordered.

32: TAKING THINGS OUT OF CONTEXT

This can work both either as an offensive strategy or a defensive strategy. Media can take a politician's statement out of context to make him or her look bad. Or, a politician can claim that he was taken out of context to, in effect, deny the meaning of what he said or to imply that the media is biased against him.

Here's an example of a Democrat PAC taking something out of context that Candidate Trump said in order to make him look bad. An ad quoted, ""You have to be wealthy in order to be great, I'm sorry to say it," with the implication that he was saying that because he was great, he was wealthy. But the context says something different.

> "During a May 26 appearance in North Dakota, on the day he secured enough delegates to clinch the Republican nomination, Trump focused on energy policy and crime rates, and how he would make the United States great again. At one point he said: "There's one more thing we have to do to make America wealthy again. And you have to be wealthy in order to be great, I'm sorry to say it." As can be seen, this attack ad takes Trump's statement out of context. He's talking about making the

country wealthy – not an individual's wealth. One could argue that Trump is too focused on associating wealth with greatness, but listening to the rest of his speech, it's clear that he was talking about increasing incomes for all Americans."[90]

On the other hand, the accusation of "that was taken out of context" can be used defensively by someone who wants to deny that something was said. The day after his treasury secretary, Steve Mnuchin, said that a weak dollar was good for the U.S. trade balance, President Trump said that Mnuchin's statement was taken out of context.[91] What he really should've said is that he (Trump) wants a stronger dollar and he's the boss. But that would've shown disagreement between the two men, so it was more politic to blame the media for supposedly taking it out of context.

Since just about everyone thinks that taking things out of context is an unfair thing to do, it is used by enemy media outlets to make a particular political candidate look bad, or by a political candidate to

---

[90] Kessler, Glenn. "Pro-Clinton group takes a Donald Trump quote out of context." Washington Post, Fact Checker, 8/23/16.

[91] Schwartz, Ian. "Pro-Clinton group takes a Donald Trump quote out of context." RealClearPolitics, 1/25/18.

make enemy media outlets look bad. Guess turnabout is fair play.

33: REPETITION DOESN'T IMPLY TRUTH

There are no Russian soldiers in Ukraine, there are no chemical weapons being used in Syria, and the ACA will eliminate millions of jobs and raise everyone's health care costs. No matter how many times these are asserted, none of these are true. For the most part they are aimed at internal audiences; Russian, Syrian and American conservatives respectively.

"There is no collusion" (tweets President Trump), over and over. This may or may not be true... we'll see what the Mueller investigation comes up with, but endless repetition is irrelevant. Sometimes governments and people just outright lie, hoping that their audience, or at least their supporters will believe them. But we've all heard the saying, "Thou doth protest too much."[92] After all, if a person is speaking the truth, why would they have to repeat it ad nauseam? Who are they trying to convince? The audience or themselves?

Scare tactics often involve saying things that aren't true. If what you say threatens or shocks enough people, it will get airplay and will be tough to counter. This is especially effective with people who won't look up the truth of the assertion, which is most of us. An example is the fictional linkage of vaccina-

---

[92] A quote from Shakespeare meaning that the speaker doubts the veracity of what another is saying.

tions with autism or retardation. Parents, understandably, have extremely protective reactions to anything that threatens the welfare of their children.

Another example is the attempt by some politicians to prevent those who don't have picture identification from voting. The guise is that there is the repeated claim of rampant voter fraud; i.e. people voting more than once by assuming someone else's identity. Some right-leaning politicians say this over and over (and over). President Trump's repeatedly stating that millions of people voted illegally have stoked this meme.[93] The facts just don't support this.

It just so happens that certain strata of people in this country are less likely to have picture identification, for a variety of reasons. These people have little to no incentive to commit voter fraud. The ratio of risk to reward for them is much too great, and they have way more important things to worry about. To disenfranchise (probably) hundreds of thousands of people from the voting process to prevent at most several hundred fraudulently cast ballots is nigh on

---

[93] There is a logical fallacy, "argumentum ad nauseam," (repeat an argument until everyone wants to barf) which fits here.

ridiculous. And partisan.[94]

Other repeated assertions are meant to stoke someone's ego. Trump maintaining, despite visual evidence to the contrary, that his inauguration crowd was bigger than Obama's would be fodder for the satirical periodical, "The Onion," if he weren't President and if he didn't make some people that surround him repeat the lie.

The upshot is that when you hear someone repeating the same thing over and over, you should automatically doubt their truth telling and question their motivation.

---

[94] On their website, the Heritage Foundation documents 1132 cases of proven voter fraud, which led to 983 criminal convictions. The violations included impersonation, duplicate voting, buying votes, fraudulent use of absentee ballots and altering the vote count. This may seem like large numbers of heinous crimes, but when one considers that these numbers represent fraud in all 50 states and elections ranging from the year 2000 to 2016, the thought that voter fraud is widespread becomes laughable.

34: ADMITTING MEANS GUILT, BUT DE-NIAL DOESN'T MEAN INNOCENCE

Older Americans will remember the Perry Mason show starring Raymond Burr. The end of each show took place in a courtroom, where Perry got the culprit to admit guilt. Likewise, in Agatha Christie mysteries, Hercule Poirot,[95] the Belgian detective, invariably gathered suspects in a sitting room, and then did "the big reveal" to accuse the perp of some dastardly crime. Of course the accused would fess up, explain how and why he committed the crime and even occasionally express contrition. My, how things have changed.

These days, there seems to be something about *not* admitting wrongdoing that makes some people think that it didn't happen, with the result that censure is avoided. Consider the "Me-Too" movement. Most people that have admitted doing something wrong have paid an appropriate price. Al Franken resigned his Senate seat. Roseann Barr, Charlie Rose and Bill O'Reilly were terminated from well-paying and notable careers. Some paid enormous sums of money to victims as recompense.

Then there are those (usually men) who just

---

[95] Poirot is the only fictional character to have an obituary written for him which appeared on the front page of the New York Times (Lask, Thomas. "Hercule Poirot Is Dead; Famed Belgian Detective." 8/6/75.

deny that they did anything wrong. Here again, President Trump repeats his role as poster child. Does anyone, for or against him, really believe that all of those women were lying? The same with Bill Cosby, once a role model for all fathers, who was accused of sexual advances (to be kind) by dozens of women. Cosby seems to have gotten his comeuppance in April, 2018, having been found guilty, but is appealing the court's decision. A third member of this cohort is "Judge" Roy Moore, who never admitted wrongdoing, but at least suffered the ignominy of losing an election to Democrat Doug Jones in the eternally Republican state of Alabama.

Trump, with galling bravado, has admitted nothing. Ever. About anything. He acts as if the "Access Hollywood" tape didn't exist, Stormy Daniels is a lying gold digger (which she may well be, but Trump certainly had an affair with her, however brief and sordid) and, of course, there was no collusion.
The phrase "deny, deny, deny" is appropriate here. Its origin can be traced to a comedic 1967 movie entitled, "A Guide For The Married Man." In it, "Joey Bishop is caught with a gal by his wife but denies everything as he calmly dresses and makes the bed. Finally sitting on his easy chair with his newspaper, he says, 'What are you talking about?' His flustered wife can only re-

spond, 'What would you like for dinner?'"[96] President Trump, Bill Cosby and Roy Moore must have studied that movie.

In the recent book by Bob Woodward, the highly respected investigative reporter who made his bones during the Watergate era, Trump is reported to advise and admonish a friend.

"Trump told the friend that it's a mistake to show weakness in the face of such accusations, according to the book. 'You've got to deny, deny, deny and push back on these women,' Trump said, according to Woodward. 'If you admit to anything and any culpability, then you're dead. That was a big mistake you made.' 'Trump said the key was showing no hesitancy in denying accusations and instead, be on the attack and push back.' 'You've got to deny anything that's said about you. Never admit.'"[97]

It would be nice if modern day offenders followed the Perry Mason and Hercule Poirot model and just admitted their sins. Since that won't happen in

[96] https://www.imdb.com/title/tt0061736/reviews

[97] Woodward, Bob. Fear: Trump in the White House. New York, Simon & Schuster, 2018.

this lifetime, we'd better get used to facing reality. If one woman were to accuse a man of unwanted sexual advances, it is reasonable to look into both sides of the story. But if many women accuse the same person of inappropriate behavior at different times, and they told other people of the occurrence soon after it happened, and that man repeatedly denies the claims, we're left with one of two choices. Either believe the accused, which means that *all* the women must be lying, or believe the women (or at least most of them) and know that the denier is a stone cold liar.

A further admonition. If we excuse the behavior of the denier in our heads because we like his policies (Trump), entertainment value (Cosby and…well, Trump again), or religiosity (Moore), realize that we are (a) condoning bad behavior which is not such a great role model for our children, (b) giving license to future perpetrators, (c) making it more difficult in the future for victims to come forward and (d) enabling autocratic tendencies, i.e. "it didn't happen because I said it didn't happen." Wake up. See bullshit for what it is…

35: AVERSION TO SCIENCE AS BULLSHIT

Every person in this country and probably every youngster who has attended school in the world has been exposed to science, starting from the git-go. In U.S. high schools, college-bound teens take four years of science. A typical sequence would be environmental science, biology, chemistry and physics between freshman and senior years. Those interested can have an extra dose of it as seniors if they choose.

Computer courses are commonly offered, ranging from becoming familiar with hardware and software to coding, programming and computer assisted design (CAD). Computers are omnipresent in schools and are encouraged at home, cost permitting, for doing assignments.

Scientists, ranging from brain surgeons to astrophysicists to molecular biologists are in high demand in twenty-first century civilization. They are some of the best and brightest, as well as the most educated people on the planet. These professions command many of the highest salaries for graduating college students.

The fruit of the labor of scientists includes radios, televisions, space exploration, computers, cell phones, miracle drugs and organ transplants. So how can anyone, in their right mind, deny anything that 99% of scientists agree on? How can anyone deny evolution or climate change? These denials involve the bending of, or avoiding of, facts which we all should consider indisputable.

If a candidate for public office believes, or says that he believes, that evolution took place within a universe created by God, that seems reasonable. If someone maintains that God created evolution, that is also reasonable. What is not acceptable is if a person maintains that evolution is "just a theory," thus implying that it may not exist. They are either ignorant to the point of being scary, or too religious to accept the scientific world we live in, or they are a candidate who is pandering to ignorant people so as to get their votes. Anyone who cannot fully and publicly back conclusive scientific evidence on a given topic should not be believed. They are either lying to get votes, bullshitting out of ignorance, or both.

Similarly, it is understandable if a candidate (or friend) says that the planet goes through heating and cooling cycles and we are currently in a heating phase. That may be true. But it's not okay if the person can't recognize the additional layer of climate change that is being added by dint of human activity. According to scientists, this is beyond debate. (And scientists, not politicians, are the ones who know about this stuff.)

We can do nothing about millennial cycles of temperature variation, but we certainly can work to make the human component less of a factor. And in any event, most scientists subscribe to the "precautionary principle," which says that if we're not sure (in the case of climate change) whether humans contribute, err on the side of assuming that we do, just in case. Those in power have a social responsibility to protect the public from possible disaster.

When Rand Paul stated that he understands that vaccines work, but that they ought to be voluntary, his assertion falls into this anti-science category. First of all, there are some things that need to be deferred to experts, in this case doctors in the aggregate. Rand Paul should know better, considering that he too is a physician. Second, if certain vaccinations are declined, children exposed to those that declined the shots may become ill. Paul said, that he had heard that some children developed profound mental disorders after being vaccinated, which was the same assertion made by Michelle Bachmann in the 2012 primaries. She, and he, have never come up with any supportive evidence. Unfortunately, this assertion, repeated endlessly because it is so shocking, gained some traction for a while. But the asserters are rarely held to account.

If any public figure does not or cannot fully and wholeheartedly support scientific evidence, they should not be believed. They are bullshitting, lying or both.

36: WHATABOUTISM AND BOTH-SIDESISM

"Whataboutism" is a logical fallacy that is aimed to counter an opponent's argument by accusing them of doing something just as bad; therefore they must be a hypocrite. It seems to have a provenance dating to the old Soviet Union. "Anyone who has ever studied the Soviet Union knows about a phenomenon called 'whataboutism.' It was the Soviet tactic of responding to Western criticism of things like Soviet human rights violations. The Soviet Union would simply reply by pointing to something the U.S. was doing wrong. The classic, cartoonish reply became: 'Oh yeah? Well you lynch Negroes.' During Putin's long and defiant reign, post-Soviet Russia has adopted this PR technique, too. It has even created an institution that is dedicated solely to the task of whataboutism. It's called Russia Today."[98][99]

Whether or not President Trump colluded with Russia before the 2016 election, it is no secret that he is an admirer (and perhaps a student) of Vladmir Putin

---

[98] Ioffe, Julia. "Kremlin TV Loves Anti-War Protests—Unless Russia Is the One Waging War." The New Republic, 3/2/14. @https://newrepublic.com/article/116816/whataboutism-russia-protests-against-war-ukraine

[99] Russia Today is a television news network which is a propaganda arm of the Russian government.

and Russian autocracy. It would be no surprise then, if he emulated standard Russian counterarguments. Whenever Trump reads or hears something new in the Mueller investigation that might affect him, he has said something like, (paraphrasing) "What about Hillary?" "Or what about the Democrats? Or Congress? Or Obama? Or the crooked media?"

An actual example is Trump's interview on the Bill O'Reilly show on FOX. When O'Reilly said that Putin is a killer, Trump responded, "There are a lot of killers. We've got a lot of killers. What do you think— our country's so innocent?"[100] Or, "How can the U.S. ever criticize Russia for bombing hospitals in Aleppo, for example, when the U.S. has killed innocents in its own errant airstrikes in the Middle East? And how could Trump, as the president of the United States, criticize the president of Russia for any of his conduct if the U.S. isn't perfect itself?"

If I were a psychologist (and I am), I might be tempted to see this as very similar to the defense mechanism of projection, wherein you "project" your own flaws or mistakes onto others, accusing them of doing what you yourself aren't proud of or are trying to hide. Projection is not foreign to Trump's modus

---

[100] Hood, Cameron. "So what about 'whataboutism'? How Trump is adopting the Russian propaganda playbook." Latterly magazine, 2/6/17. @https://medium.com/latterly/so-what-about-whataboutism-497b08213b8

operandi. When questioned about the wisdom of pardoning Sheriff Joe Arpaio, a convicted felon, Trump responded by questioning pardons granted by Clinton and Obama. These pardons may not have been the greatest ideas, but that is a discussion for another time. The Arpaio pardon stunk on its own "merits."

With the rise in tribalism in the last few years, whataboutism has increased commensurately. It's not a one-sided method. When confronted with hard evidence of Trump's lying, many of his loyal supporters, rather than deal with the lies, simply have said, "Well, the Democrats are worse," which is another version of whataboutism. And when asked why they would vote for Hillary, a less than inspiring candidate, many Democrats would reply, "Well, Trump is worse."

Whataboutism is an excellent strategy for deflection and changing the subject. Kelly Anne Conway, a Trump representative, is a master of this. In the campaign, she appeared on any television network show that would have her. She regularly frustrated interviewers, since whenever her boss was criticized, she would riff on the failings of Hillary Clinton or the Democrats, or the media, or anyone else aside from Donald Trump. To her credit, she was really, really good at this and, I believe, was so maddening to some television hosts, that they stopped inviting her to appear on their shows.

A final related fallacy is "bothsidesism," also called "false equivalence," which Paul Krugman has been railing against since the advent of Donald Trump's campaign for the Presidency began.

> "...some reporters and news organizations try to point out Trump statements that are false, frightening, or both. All too often, however, they still try to maintain their treasured balance by devoting equal time — and, as far as readers and viewers can tell, equal or greater passion — to denouncing far less important misstatements from Hillary Clinton. In fact, surveys show that Mrs. Clinton has, overall, received much more negative coverage than her opponent.
> And in the last few days we've seen a spectacular demonstration of bothsidesism in action: an op-ed article from the incoming and outgoing heads of the White House Correspondents' Association, with the headline "Trump, Clinton both threaten free press." How so? Well, Mr. Trump has selectively banned news organizations he considers hostile; he has also, although the op-ed didn't mention it, attacked both those organizations and

individual reporters, and refused to condemn supporters who, for example, have harassed reporters with anti-Semitic insults.

Meanwhile, while Mrs. Clinton hasn't done any of these things, and has a staff that readily responds to fact-checking questions, she doesn't like to hold press conferences. Equivalence!"[101]

The most famous example of bothsidesism in recent years was President Trump's statement regarding the Charlottesville, Virginia protests. "'I think there is blame on both sides,' the President said in a combative exchange with reporters at Trump Tower in Manhattan. 'You had a group on one side that was bad. You had a group on the other side that was also very violent. Nobody wants to say that. I'll say it right now.'"[102] Trump has been raked over the coals for that one, but his supporters may be relieved to know that David Duke (who is known as a white supremacist, an antisemite, a conspiracy theorist, a convicted felon

---

[101] Krugman, Paul. "Both Sides Now?" New York Times Op-Ed, 7/18/16.

[102] Shear, Michael D. & Haberman, Maggie. "Trump Defends Initial Remarks on Charlottesville; Again Blames 'Both Sides'." New York Times, 8/15/17.

and an ex-Grand Wizard of the K.K.K.) is very much in his corner.

The commonality among whataboutism, both-sidesism and false equivalence is the attempt to change the conversation to something not related to the original topic. If your opponent can distract, deflect and/or obfuscate what you were trying to say, you've lost and your opponent has won. For the independent listener, whenever someone says, "Okay, but what about _____," or "Both sides have equal value," you should stop and do your own evaluation. Occasionally, the arguments on both sides will actually have equal validity, but if so, it should be obvious. If someone has to say that they are equal, they probably aren't.

37: BLOWING SMOKE UP YOUR ASS (TELL 'EM WHAT THEY WANT TO HEAR)

The Urban Dictionary defines "blowing smoke up your ass" as: People who constantly tell you what you WANT to hear ...Feeding someone's ego with constant adoration and commentary. Telling someone everything they want to hear and nothing they need to hear.[103]

> You are a loving husband in a good marriage. Your wife comes downstairs after having gone to the hairdresser earlier in the day. She says, "George, did you notice my hair?" You reply, " It looks great Honey (as you push down your gag reflex)! I love those little curls (that make her look like her head was caught in washing machine)!
>
> You are a loving wife. George, your husband, tells a stupid, childish joke that you've heard ten times before. You, Marilyn, say, "George, I laugh every time you tell that one (as you turn your back to roll your eyes)! You haven't lost your sense of

[103] https://www.urbandictionary.com/define.php?term=blowing%20smoke%20up%20your%20ass

humor after all these years (of course you never had one to lose)."

You are a car salesman. "Mr. Peters, you have good taste. That's our most popular model." Mr Peters: "Does it get good mileage?" "Good question, you reply... you seem to be an educated consumer."

You are a political candidate giving a speech in a state where manufacturing jobs are disappearing. "Ladies and Gentlemen, we have to bring jobs back to this state. Your main products are coal and steel. So we're going to push through supplements to the coal industry so that they can hire more miners. And with that coal, we're going to produce more steel so that jobs expand there too! And we'll put tariffs on foreign steel, so that our companies become more competitive. After all, China is illegally flooding the market with cheap steel."

This is usually pure bullshit, as opposed to lies, since the smoke-blower doesn't care what is true or not. For example, George may or may not have liked his wife's hair but is obligated to tell how nice it is regardless of his real opinion. If he doesn't, he's in deep caca. Candidates have to tell their audiences what they want to hear. That is, if they want their audience not to leave before their speech is over or vote for their opponent.

This type of bullshit is usually harmless, except when the audience *badly needs* to believe what the speaker is saying. For example, if I am a coal or steel worker who is afraid of losing my job and income, I want any candidate who promises a reprieve. The problem is that these promises rarely come true, but the victims don't find out until much later. This is why many are turned off to politics, and why the phrase "drain the swamp" has become a meme. People are sick of the swamp creatures that have promised them things in the past. Unfortunately, it's difficult to identify the really bad swamp creatures from the not-so-bad ones. Often the really bad swamp creatures are the ones warning the public about the really bad swamp creatures.

As with other types of advertisers, promises made by politicians need to be taken with a large grain of salt. Their goal is to get elected. They know what you need and are sorely tempted to sculpt what they say to those needs, regardless of whether what they promise is likely or even possible.

38: DATA POINTS

Having had a lot of math and science courses as well as ones in psychology, I am tuned in to what can be called "behavioral data points"; that is, trends in the behavior of people that allow the summarizing of a person's style or modus operandi. I'm not alone in seeking out data points. Facebook and Google make billions by selling ads targeted to, as an example, veterans, by using patriotic memes, the flag and pictures of men who have served. Or to teens by targeting to those who like certain bands or brands of apparel. (I haven't figured out how to make billions myself, however.)

Organizations also use data points to evaluate the loyalty of certain politicians. The National Rifle Association rates legislators from A+ to F, depending on the ways that they voted on the single issue of gun rights and support for the Second Amendment. An organization named "Progressive Punch" gives ratings of the percent of issues on which a legislator supports progressive views. (They range from Kamala Harris of California, who supports progressive legislation roughly 99% of the time to Cindy Hyde-Smith from Mississippi, who has never supported progressive causes.)[104]

---

[104] https://progressivepunch.org/scores.htm?house=senate

Politicians can be typecast by data points as well. Consider Mitt Romney, the 2012 Republican candidate for President. In private school, he was the ringleader of a group of boys that bullied a classmate by holding him down and cutting off his long hair. In the Republican debates, Romney made comments such as "I'll bet you $10,000," "middle income is $200,000 to $250,000," "I'm not concerned about the very poor. We have a safety net," "my house in California has a car elevator," "Ann [his wife] drives a couple of Cadillacs."[105] And who can forget the "47%" comment made at a fundraiser. We're not talking about one gaffe or misstatement. We're presented with a series of behaviors (or data points), mostly verbal, that indicate Romney's sense of entitlement and the implied lack of being able to identify with those less fortunate. His wealth and his attitude toward those with less was surely a contributor to his election loss.

The different, but just as indelible, meme seems to have evolved around Hillary Clinton and her husband. The Clintons were stereotyped as having a sense of entitlement and perhaps acting as if they were above the law. The main piece of data here is Hillary's use of a single email account, the contents of which were housed on server in her home, which she

---

[105] Numbers quoted are approximates.

refused to hand over to enquiring bodies (meaning Republicans). Other data points stem back to the Whitewater investigation and Bill Clinton's affairs, which also had an effect on her reputation.

Since the onset of the Presidential race that culminated in the 2016 election, the new meme, the new normal, is the ubiquity and omnipresence of bullshit and lies. And as easy as it was to ascribe data points to Romney and Clinton, the consistency of President Trump's behavior, which has been faithfully documented by reliable sources, provide data points that should not and cannot be ignored.

I realize, that as a psychologist, I'm going to look for these personality traits or trends, but *it will behoove every prospective voter to look for consistent behaviors in a candidate that either enhance or detract from their candidacy.*

39: THE BULLSHIT EQUATIONS

Bullshit, as well as lies, can range from being merely laughable to quite effective. Both can also do anywhere from no damage to tons of it. What follows is an attempt to develop formulas to measure the degree to which bullshit is effective and how much damage it causes. To begin, it is assumed that truth is good, and bullshitting, lying or some combination thereof is bad. First we'll define the variables that bear on the effectiveness of the bullshit.

Power (P): Power is a property of the bullshitter. Things that contribute to the power of the bullshit are the status (S), likability (L) and charisma (C) of the bullshitter. It is proposed that Power (P) is a function of the status of the bullshitter multiplied by the sum of his likability and charisma. Thus...

$$P = fn (S \times (L + C))$$

The equation implies that as the status of the bullshitter approaches zero, the product of **(S x (L + C))**, and thus his or her power also approaches zero. If the bullshitter is neither likable not charismatic, the sum of **L** and **C** is approaches zero, as does the product of **(S x (L + C))**, so the Power is zero.

It should be obvious that if the bullshitter has no status, is unlikable and lacks charisma, that very few, if any, people will believe what he or she says. People having status will be believed out of fear. Examples are a police officer, an autocrat or, perhaps, even a fire-and-brimstone preacher. Those who are charismatic or likable will lead people to *want* to believe them. The advertisers that hired Matthew McConaughey to sell Lincolns, LeBron James to sell Kias, and Jennifer Garner and Samuel Jackson hocking credit cards, ascribe to this principle.

On occasion a bullshitter will possess all three qualities. At other times, a person may have status, but be lacking in one or both likability or charisma. Putin has status and some charisma, but not so much likability, George W. Bush had status and likability, but not so much charisma, Obama had status and charisma, but many found him unlikable. A salesman may have either likability or charisma, but has little status. Successful bullshitters will usually have all three (S, L & C) by degrees.

Vulnerability (V): Vulnerability is a property of the ones being bullshat, or the bullshittees or the audience. The more vulnerable the target audience, the more the victim *wants* or *needs* to believe the bullshit. Vulnerability, in turn, can be broken down into three categories. First is the degree of desperation (D). A person whose life is not going well in terms of employment or finances needs hope, and will tend to believe anyone who gives it to him. The hope-giver fills the role of savior.

A second part of vulnerability involves people who need a scapegoat. Often these people are prejudiced (PR) and / or feel that other groups are displacing them (such as minorities), or taking advantage of them ("intellectual elites").

The third contributor to vulnerability, which may be somewhat correlated with the first two, is limited intelligence (LI). The less bright a person, the less they can or will question, or see through, the bullshit. Further, since their attitudes are based on belief rather than reasoned analysis, they will be less open to changing their minds.

Vulnerability is projected to be an additive function of the three components: desperation (D), prejudice (PR) and limited intelligence (LI). Thus...

$$V = fn \ (D + PR + LI)$$

Those who are financially secure, and thus not desperate, who are not prejudiced (by degrees, of course) and thus are not threatened by "the other," and are intelligent enough to reason through complex issues, will not be very vulnerable to bullshit. The sum of **(D + PR + LI)** will approach zero, as will vulnerability.

People who have lost their jobs due to automation may be desperate, but not necessarily prejudiced or of limited intelligence. A person who is desperate to be married will be more vulnerable to a bullshitting beau or girlfriend. Some who still have jobs but are afraid of being displaced by minorities may be prejudiced, but not necessarily desperate or of limited intelligence. In sales situations, the only one of these three categories that makes a potential buyer vulnerable is limited intelligence; that is, they will be easier to "trick" into falling for a sales pitch. Vulnerable people will usually have some combination of these three categories (D, PR & LI) by degrees.

Self-interest (SI): Most vulnerable people are open to believing bullshit because the bullshit serves what we've called Protective Self-Interest in that it offers them hope of getting a job and supporting their families, protects them from "the other" that want to take their jobs away, and allows them to not have to deal with the complexities of financial and political issues.

Bullshitters that promise to increase the wealth or power of the audience appeal to a different kind of self-interest, what we call Direct Self-Interest, or what can also be called greed. The bullshit may be well received, whether or not the audience actually believes it. They will go along with it even though they know it is bullshit because it benefits them in some way. They "wink-wink" at it, or ignore the odiousness of the bullshitter because it serves their needs.

Thus, some fortunate souls will benefit from a rise in the stock market, or tax cuts for the wealthy, or rules that favor industry over the environment. They may see the bullshit for what it is, or come to believe the bullshit because they profit from it.

Effectiveness of the Bullshit (E): Effectiveness will be a function of the three variables defined above, namely the power of the bullshitter, the vulnerability of the audience and the self-interest satisfied in the audience. Thus…

$$E = fn\ ((P \times V) + SI)$$

If P and V are both high, that is, a powerful person is bullshitting to a vulnerable audience, it is quite likely that the bullshit will be quite effective, regardless of the self-interest to the audience.

If either P or V approaches zero (e.g. are very low), their product will be low (since any number times zero is zero), so that the believability of the bullshit will depend on whether it serves the self-interest of the audience. Wealthy people fit here.

If P is high, but V and SI are low, the audience will see through the bullshit and not believe it, even if it is coming from a very powerful person. A well educated, non-desperate or prejudiced person who does not overly benefit from the bullshit, fits here.

If V is high, but P and SI are low, a very vulnerable person may seek out the bullshit of a not very powerful person, such as a cult leader, because they need something or someone to believe in.

The **Damage** done by bullshit is dependent on three variables. The first, the effectiveness of the bullshit E, was defined above. The other two are the **number** of people that the bullshit reaches, N, and the **importance** of the subject, I.

$$DMG = E \times N \times I$$

Damage done is a product of the effectiveness of the bullshit, the number of people reached and the importance of the subject. If any of E, N or I approach zero, the damage done approaches zero. By example, if the bullshit is not effective or the number of people reached is small, then the damage done will be minimal, regardless of the importance of the topic.

40: TAKEAWAYS

1...Claiming "fake news" is an all-around, vague response to anything disagreed with when the asserter has no reasonable defense. Thus, whenever it is invoked, "fake news" is clearly and undoubtedly a poster child for BULLSHIT!

2... If you believe bullshit, it says something about you. If you are wise enough to see through the bullshit, it will tell you a lot about the person who is bullshitting.

3... If your sink is leaking, don't call an intellectual. If you need to understand a complex societal issue, don't call a plumber. If you want to know the truth, don't call a bullshit artist. Understand what you know and know what you understand. What you know has limits, so know those limits. If you don't know what you don't know you will likely be a victim of bullshit and, too boot, end up repeating it.

4... The first task of the listener is to recognize bullshit when she hears it. The second is to figure out the motivation or agenda of the bullshitter.

5... Major tools of a bullshit artist are distraction and deflection. A truth teller doesn't need to avoid the subject at hand. If someone changes the subject, you are on their turf and at a disadvantage. You must recognize the deflection, point it out and return the conversation to the original subject.

6… If a story sounds unlikely in the extreme, it is probably bullshit.

7… We are all logical creatures, but what enters into our logical processes are merely beliefs, which can be true, false or any place in between. So if we don't agree with someone else's conclusions, they can be logical but operating on false premises. Remember the phrase, "garbage in, garbage out."

8… To counter an argument where someone cherry picks their examples, learn to ask for proof, and inquire about the number of people being referenced (sample size) and whether or not those people were randomly selected.

9… If what another person says is irrelevant to the subject under discussion, call him or her on it.

10… We all live in our own echo chambers, taking in information that agrees with what we believe, and avoiding or rejecting that which is dissonant. This is confirmation bias, and we are all guilty of it. We should therefore question our own beliefs on occasion.

11… When someone who has a hardened belief is confronted with proof that the belief is false, they will pull in correlated beliefs, also called rationalizations, so as to be able to maintain that hardened belief. An example is when the N.R.A. is confronted with incident after incident of gun violence, they will claim, "People kill people, guns don't," or "It's a mental health problem," or "Next, they'll be coming after all our guns." This allows them to oppose any gun control measures in the face of mass shootings.

12… People need to have hope, so if they are suffering they will trust in and believe someone who promises relief. Those in need are easy targets of bullshit artists and liars. Without fact checking, these hopeful people become repeaters of bullshit. This is called "drinking the Kool-Aid."

13… People who feel looked down upon by intellectual elitists are more vulnerable to a "regular guy" who is charismatic. What this regular guy represents may be anywhere from truth to bullshit.

14… We all bullshit and lie, by degrees. And we are all victims of bullshit and lies, again by degrees.

15… Bullshitters do so to get what they want and/or protect themselves from something they don't want. The listener should try to figure out the motivation that lies behind the bullshit.

16… Bullshit is much easier to spread than it is to refute because very few people have the desire, time or ability to check the facts.

17… Technology makes bullshitting and lying easier and multiplies their effects. Bullshitting or lying at a distance has next to no negative consequences. The bullshitter doesn't have to face his victim.

18… Bullshit allows reputations to be sculpted rather than earned.

19… The earlier in life a person learns to filter bullshit, the less vulnerable they will be to it later in life. Teach logic, critical thinking and filtering techniques as early as possible.

20… In personal relationships, liars ruin trust, while bullshitters are merely annoying since we can usually see through them. In sales and advertising, bullshit is expected and fairly easily filtered out. In politics, we sometimes need to believe that help is on the way, so that we are open to being bamboozled.

21... Many situations demand or require bullshit. No one will buy a mediocre product, so what I'm selling has to be the best, or else I'm toast. No one will vote for a politician who tells the truth and delivers bad news. Bullshit is the order of the day and once it flies, flip-flopping is kryptonite to a campaign.

22... The damage done by bullshit will vary with the power of the bullshitter, the vulnerability of the audience, the number of people reached and the importance of the subject.

23... When someone in power bullshits frequently, it gives license to everyone beneath him or her to act similarly. This is the same as if parents drink heavily or use drugs, their teenagers may feel they have license to do the same.

24... If someone discounts a statement because of any personal characteristic such as gender, race or ethnicity, that is bullshit. A statement should stand or fall on its merits. The word "irrelevant" is a good fit here.

25... If someone says, "Some people are saying..." or "I've heard that...," the listener should immediately ask, "Which people are saying?" "Or who told you that?" If no answer in forthcoming it is almost certainly bullshit.

26… If a person says that they are the only one who can solve your problem, that's bullshit. No one is omnipotent.

27… Consider the source of the statement. Does that person have credibility in the field? LeBron has cred in basketball, not cars. Doctors have credibility about medical topics. Trump has credibility in real estate, and not much else.

28… If you are being told that, "new is better," or "old is better," or "natural is better," do some research before you buy that argument. They are not necessarily true.

29… Flattery will get you anywhere. Be wary of people blowing smoke up your ass. If you are being flattered, the other person wants something from you, might want to curry favor from you for another purpose, or wants you to do something that's good for them, but not necessarily good for you. It's usually bullshit.

30... If a politician is saying things with which no one can disagree, it is bullshit and meaningless.

31... Conspiracy theories are almost always bullshit. Theorists put together random facts to concoct a story that fits a particular agenda. Ask for proof, which won't be available. If there were actual proof, it wouldn't be a conspiracy theory, it would be a real story.

32... Scare tactics are often related to conspiracy theories. If you vaccinate your child, he will be autistic. If we let immigrants in, they will rape and pillage. Muslims will all be terrorists. And Elvis lives.

33... Competition ensures that the mainstream media provides relatively accurate information. The most talented people compete, as do athletes, to make it to the highest levels. Reporters and owners of esteemed periodicals/networks will not risk their reputation, careers or businesses by spreading "fake news." It is the ones who have low costs (i.e., no reputation to lose) and high rewards (making network coverage) who will offer fake news.

34... Aversion to science and/or denial of scientific findings is bullshit, pure and simple. As with the reporting of news, competition among universities and scientists ensures that widely accepted scientific conclusions are the closest thing to truth that exists.

35… If a person concludes an argument with what he started with, it is circular and needs to be ignored. "The Mueller investigation is biased, so we must ignore the findings because they will be against the President." Assuming bias starts the circularity.

36… Correlation doesn't mean causation. If something good happens on my watch, it doesn't mean I deserve credit. Nor can I necessarily be blamed if something bad happens on my watch.

37… Claiming something over and over doesn't mean it is true. Stating a belief emotionally also doesn't mean it is true.

38… Admitting does imply guilt. The tactic of "deny, deny, deny" doesn't guarantee innocence.

39… If you hear a snippet of a speech that seems slanted, listen to more of the speech to evaluate for yourself as to whether the reporting should have been more balanced.

40… If someone is always calling something or someone the greatest or the worst, they are probably speaking hyperbolically, i.e. exaggerating, and therefore should be taken with a grain of salt. Most people and actions are on a gray scale… neither the greatest nor the worst.

41… If you complain about what your spouse has done to you, and she responds by saying, "But what about what you did to me?," that is "whataboutism." This changes the subject and you should point that out.

42… If someone tries to assign equal blame to two sides in an argument (aka "bothsidesism"), evaluate whether equal blame is appropriate. Reference Donald Trump's equating the white nationalist protesters with others who were protesting Confederate monuments in Charlottesville, Virginia in 2017.

43… Data points don't lie. If a person has been a bully, or a sneak or a bullshitter most of his or her life, don't expect future behavior to be different. Leopards don't change their spots. And as a psychologist, I know that you can help someone to change a little, but I can't make a prince out of a frog.

44… The "Bully Pulpit" can be used for noble causes or ignoble ones. It can be used to reassure the populace, or spread bullshit. Recall:

"The only thing we have to fear is fear itself…" (F.D.R.)

"Ask not what your country can do for you. Ask what you can do for your country." (J.F.K.)

"Mr. Gorbachev, tear down this wall!" (Ronald Reagan)

"A house divided against itself cannot stand." (Abe Lincoln)

"Despite the negative press covfefe," (Donald Trump)

REFERENCES

Anderson, Carol. "The Republican Approach to Voter Fraud: Lie. New York Times Op-Ed, 9/8/18.

Belluz, Julia. "Dr. Oz is a quack. Now Trump's appointing him to be a health adviser." Vox, 5/4/18.

Brandolini, Alberto. @ http://ordrespontane.blogspot.fr/2014/07/brandolinis-law.html2

Cilizza, Chris. "President Trump lied more than 3,000 times in 466 days." CNN Politics, 5/9/18 @https://www.cnn.com/2018/05/01/politics/donald-trump-3000/index.html

Cooper, Marta. "Donald Trump's great, tremendous, unbelievable penchant for hyperbole at the first presidential debate." Quartz, 9/27/16. @https://qz.com/792825/presidential-debate-donald-trumps-great-tremendous-unbelievable-penchant-for-hyperbole/

Crabtree, Michael. "New Poll Gauges Americans' General Knowledge Levels." news.gallup,com, 7/6/1999.

Daru, Deena, "Robert De Niro unleashes profanity-laced rant against Trump." CNN Politics, 1/10/18.

Edelman, Ric. @ https://www.edelmanfinancial.com/financial-planning/to-buy-cars-and-homes

Egan, Timothy. "Trickle Down Trumpsters and the Debasement of Language." New York Times Op-Ed, 6/22/18.

Epps, Garrett. "Ted Cruz Is a Natural- Born Citizen" The Atlantic, 1/14/16.

Frankfurt, Harry G. On Bullshit. Princeton, N.J.: Princeton University Press, 2005.

French, David. "Mueller's Investigation Won't Shake Trump's
Base." New York Times, Op-Ed, 10/30/17.

Gilmore, Scott. "The definitive list of every person Donald
Trump has called a loser." MacLean's, 7/21/15.

Gribin, Anthony J. Selfonomics: How Broadly Defined Self-Interest Explains Everything. ttgPress, 2013.

Gribin, Anthony. Trump's Tricks: The Artful Use of Intimidation and Lies. ttgPress, 2016.

Gribin, Anthony. I Am An Echo Chamber: The Basis of Tribalism. ttgPress, 2018.

Hannity, Sean (staff). "BUSTED! NY Times Suggests Nikki Haley Bought $52k Curtains, Actually Purchased by Obama Ad-
min." At: https://www.hannity.com/media-room/busted-ny-
times-suggests-nikki-haley-bought-52k-curtains-actually-pur-
chased-by-obama-admin/

Heer, Jeet. "Worse Than a Liar." The New Republic, 3/15/18.
@https://newrepublic.com/article/147504/worse-liar-trump-
lies-trudeau

Hood, Cameron. "So what about 'whataboutism'? How Trump
is adopting the Russian propaganda playbook." Latterly maga-

zine, 2/6/17. @https://medium.com/latterly/so-what-about-whataboutism-497b08213b8

http://2012election.procon.org/view.source-summary-chart.php

http://www.historynet.com/causes-of-the-civil-war

https://www.imdb.com/title/tt0061736/reviews

https://www.brainyquote.com/search_results?q=honesty

https://mediabiasfactcheck.com/2016/07/20/the-10-best-fact-checking-sites/

https://www.collegefactual.com/majors/communication-journalism-media/journalism/rankings/top-ranked/

https://progressivepunch.org/scores.htm?house=senate

Ioffe, Julia. "Kremlin TV Loves Anti-War Protests—Unless Russia Is the One Waging War." The New Republic, 3/2/14. @https://newrepublic.com/article/116816/whataboutism-russia-protests-against-war-ukraine

Jarrett, Gregg. "Robert Mueller and his politically biased team of prosecutors need to go." Fox News, Politics, 12/9/17.

Katz, David L. "Is Organic Food Better?" U.S. News Health, 9/4/2012.

Kessler, Glenn. "Pro-Clinton group takes a Donald Trump quote out of context." Washington Post, Fact Checker, 8/23/16.

Krieg, Gregory. "10 of the most questionable things Trump's claimed credit for." CNN Politics, 1/2/18. https://www.cnn.com/2018/01/02/politics/donald-trump-took-credit-for-what/index.html

Kristof, Nicholas. "Our Addiction to Trump." New York Times Op-Ed, 5/5/18. Lang, Nico. "14 Surprising Things Americans Don't Know, According To Poll Numbers." 10/7/13. thought-catalog.com.

Krugman, Paul. "Both Sides Now?" New York Times Op-Ed, 7/18/16.

Lask, Thomas. "Hercule Poirot Is Dead; Famed Belgian Detective." 8/6/75.

Lattman, Stewart. "The Origins of Justice Stewart's "I Know It When I See It." Wall Street Journal, Law Blog, 9/27/07.

Malone, Scott. "Trump's profanity delights supporters, horrifies etiquette experts." Reuters, 1/12/18.

Marcus, Ruth. "Trump said, 'I alone can fix it.' How wrong he was." Washington Post, 1/20/18.

Marie-Claire magazine, May 4, 2016. http://www.marieclaire.co.uk/ blogs/550112/donald-trump-quotes.html#yWAf1ip3D0y8Hr0H.99

Mark, Michelle. "Trump just referred to one of his most infamous campaign comments: calling Mexicans 'rapists'." Business Insider, 4/5/18.

Moore, David W. "Nine of Ten Americans View Smoking as Harmful." news.gallup.com, 10/7/1999.

Munnell, Alicia H. "Fiduciary rule takes a hit in the Fifth Circuit." marketwatch, 4/12/18.

Nowrasteh, Alex. "Immigration and Crime – What the Research Says." CATO Institute, 7/14/15. @https://www.cato.org/blog/immigration-crime-what-research-says

Oehlheiser, Amy. "This is how Facebook's fake-news writers make money." Washington Post, 11/18/16.

Peele, Stanton. "Bullshitting: Lessons from the Masters,How the great bullshitters pull it off." Psychology Today, first posted May 15, 2009. @https://www.psychologytoday.com/us/blog/addiction-in-society/200905/bullshitting-lessons-the-masters

Samuelsohn, Darren. "A guide to Donald Trump's 'rigged' election: Zombie Democrats, colluding reporters and backstabbing Republicans. Politico, 10/25/16.

Schwartz, Ian. "Pro-Clinton group takes a Donald Trump quote out of context." RealClearPolitics, 1/25/18.

Shapiro, Leslie. "Anatomy of a Russian Facebook ad." Washington Post, Business Analysis, 11/1/17.

Shear, Michael D. & Haberman, Maggie. "Trump Defends Initial Remarks on Charlottesville; Again Blames 'Both Sides'." New York Times, 8/15/17.

Speake, Jennifer. Oxford Dictionary of Proverbs. London, Oxford University Press, 2015 (6th ed.).

Ward, Megan. Prezi @ https://prezi.com/wj7woufp9srz/logical-fallacies-within-advertisements/

Weems, Mason Locke. "The Fable of George Washington and the Cherry Tree." From The Life of George Washington, 1809.

Wemple, Erik. "New York Times wrongs Nikki Haley with curtain headline." Washington Post Op-Ed, 9/14/18

Wending, Mike. "The (almost) complete history of 'fake news.'" BBC News, 1/22/18.

Wolf, Leon H. "Called it: Trump Implies that Hillary Clinton Killed Vince Foster." Red State (newsletter), 5/23/16.

Zadrozny, Brandy & Collins, Ben. "How three conspiracy theorists took 'Q' and sparked Qanon. NBC News, 8/14/18. https://www.nbcnews.com/tech/tech-news/how-three-conspiracy-theorists-took-q-sparked-qanon-n900531.

www.ingramcontent.com/pod-product-compliance
Lightning Source LLC
Chambersburg PA
CBHW031506270326
41930CB00006B/268